ENGLISH

Curriculum **Bank** 1811507.

KEY STAGE ONE
SCOTTISH LEVELS A-B

POETRY

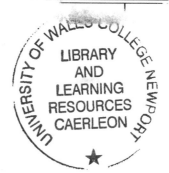

MOIRA ANDREW

Published by Scholastic Ltd,
Villiers House,
Clarendon Avenue,
Leamington Spa,
Warwickshire CV32 5PR
Text © Moira Andrew
© 1999 Scholastic Ltd
1 2 3 4 5 6 7 8 9 0 9 0 1 2 3 4 5 6 7 8

AUTHOR
MOIRA ANDREW

EDITOR
JOEL LANE

ASSISTANT EDITOR
KATE PEARCE

SERIES DESIGNER
LYNNE JOESBURY

DESIGNER
SARAH ROCK

ILLUSTRATIONS
GARRY DAVIES

COVER ILLUSTRATION
JONATHAN BENTLEY

INFORMATION TECHNOLOGY CONSULTANT
MARTIN BLOWS

SCOTTISH 5–14 LINKS
MARGARET SCOTT AND SUSAN GOW

Designed using Adobe Pagemaker

British Library Cataloguing-in-Publication Data
A catalogue record for this book is available from the
British Library.

ISBN 0-590-53786-5

Contents

INTRODUCTION	**5**
Overview grid	13
READING AND SHARING	**17**
WRITING POEMS	**47**
USING A PATTERN	**67**
PLAYING WITH FORMS	**89**
PHOTOCOPIABLES	**107**
IT links	158
Cross-curricular links	160

ACKNOWLEDGEMENTS

The publishers gratefully acknowledge permission to reproduce the following copyright material:

Moira Andrew for the use of 'Who lives here?', 'Picnic-packaged' and 'Cake for tea', all previously unpublished © 1999, Moira Andrew; 'I like' from *Senses Poems* ed. John Foster © 1996, Moira Andrew (1996, *More Conkers* series, Oxford Reading Tree, OUP); 'In one second' from *Paint A Poem* by Moira Andrew © 1996, Moira Andrew (1996, Belair); 'Breakfast boast' from *Hammy's House* ed. John Foster © 1992, Moira Andrew (1992, OUP); 'Shower' from *The First Lick of the Lolly* ed. Moira Andrew © 1986, Moira Andrew (1986, Macmillan Educational).

John Coldwell for the use of 'Eataweek' by John Foster from *Crack Another Yolk* ed. John Foster © 1996, John Coldwell (1996, OUP).

John Cotton for the use of 'The week' by John Cotton from *First Things* by John Cotton © 1993, John Cotton (1993, Nelson); 'Riddle of summer' from *Language in Colour* ed. Moira Andrew © 1989, John Cotton (1989, Belair); 'First Things' from *The First Lick of the Lolly* ed. Moira Andrew © 1986, John Cotton (1986, Macmillan Educational).

Egmont Children's Books for the use of 'Countdown' by Jack Prelutsky from *It's Halloween* by Jack Prelutsky © 1978, Jack Prelutsky (1978, Mammoth; published by William Heinemann, a division of Egmont Children's Books Ltd).

John Fairfax for the use of 'A-Z of Beasts and Eats' from *Read A Poem, Write A Poem* ed. Wes Magee © 1989, John Fairfax (1989, Blackwell).

John Foster for the use of 'When the wind blows' by John Foster from *Language in Colour* ed. Moira Andrew © 1989, John Foster (1989, Belair); 'Says of the week' from *Four O'Clock Friday* by John Foster © 1991, John Foster (1991, OUP).

HarperCollins Publishers for the use of 'A Small Dragon' by Brian Patten from *Notes To The Hurrying Man* by Brian Patten © 1980 Brian Patten (Geo. Allen and Unwin).

David Higham Associates for 'The Secret Brother' by Elizabeth Jennings from *The Secret Brother* by Elizabeth Jennings © 1966, Elizabeth Jennings (1966, 1997, Macmillan).

Richard James for the use of his poem 'Kitchen Sounds' from *Senses Poems* ed. John Foster © 1996, Richard James (1996, *More Conkers* series, Oxford Reading Tree, OUP).

Jean Kenward for the use of 'Colours' by Jean Kenward from *The Wider World* ed. Robyn Gordon © 1998, Jean Kenward (1998, Riverpoint Publishing).

Wes Magee for the use of 'Climb the mountain' from *Witch's Brew and Other Poems* by Wes Magee © 1989, Wes Magee (1989, Cambridge University Press).

Judith Nicholls for the use of the poems 'Timeless' and 'Magic' by Judith Nicholls from *Dragonsfire* by Judith Nicholls © 1990, Judith Nicholls (1990, Faber & Faber); 'Sack Race' by Judith Nicholls from *Higgledy-Humbug* by Judith Nicholls © 1990, Judith Nicholls (1990, Mary Glasgow Publications); 'When?' by Judith Nicholls from *A Blue Poetry Paintbox* ed. John Foster © 1994, Judith Nicholls (1994, OUP) and 'Breakfast for one' by Judith Nicholls from *The First Lick of the Lolly* ed. Moira Andrew © 1986, Judith Nicholls (1986, Macmillan Educational).

Peters, Fraser & Dunlop on behalf of the author for the use of 'The hardest thing in the world to do' by Michael Rosen from *You Tell Me* by Michael Rosen © 1979, Michael Rosen (1979, Penguin Books); 'Say please' by Michael Rosen from *The First Lick of the Lolly* ed. Moira Andrew © 1986, Michael Rosen (1986, Macmillan Educational).

Marian Reiner, Literary Agent, New York, for the author for permission to use 'Weather is full of the nicest sounds' by Aileen Fisher from *I Like Weather* by Aileen Fisher © 1963, renewed 1991, Aileen Fisher.

John Rice for the use of 'Mettle Fettle' from *Scholastic Collections: Poetry* compiled by Wes Magee © 1992, John Rice (1992, Scholastic Limited).

The Society of Authors as the representative for the Literary Trustees of Walter de la Mare for the use of 'The Cupboard' by Walter de la Mare, originally from *Peacock Pie* (1913) and from *The Complete Poems of Walter de la Mare* © 1969, Walter de la Mare.

Ian Souter for 'Storm trouble' by Ian Souter from *Another Very First Poetry Book* ed. John Foster © 1992, Ian Souter (1992, OUP).

John Walsh for the use of 'Snow-stroll' by John Walsh from *Rainbow Year* ed. Moira Andrew © 1994, John Walsh (1994, Belair).

Colin West for the use of three verses from 'Wild Flowers' and for 'Home' from *A Moment In Rhyme* by Colin West © 1987, Colin West (1987, Hutchinson).

David Whitehead for the use of 'Easy Peasy' from *Somewhere in the Sky* ed. Moira Andrew © 1996, David Whitehead (1996, Nelson).

Irene Yates for the use of 'Harvest Festival' first published in *Infant Projects* magazine No. 60 1988 © 1988, Irene Yates (1988, Scholastic Limited).

Introduction

Scholastic Curriculum Bank is a series for all primary teachers, providing an essential planning tool for devising comprehensive schemes of work as well as an easily accessible and varied bank of practical, classroom-tested activities with photocopiable resources.

Designed to help planning for and implementation of progression, differentiation and assessment, *Scholastic Curriculum Bank* offers a structured range of stimulating activities with clearly stated learning objectives that reflect the programmes of study, and detailed lesson plans that allow busy teachers to put ideas into practice with the minimum amount of preparation time. The photocopiable sheets that accompany many of the activities provide ways of integrating purposeful application of knowledge and skills, differentiation, assessment and record-keeping.

Opportunities for formative assessment are highlighted within the activities where appropriate, while separate summative assessment activities give guidelines for analysis and subsequent action. Ways of using information technology for different purposes and in different contexts, as a tool for communicating and handling information and as a means of investigating, are integrated into the activities where appropriate, and more explicit guidance is provided at the end of the book.

The series covers all the primary curriculum subjects, with separate books for Key Stages 1 and 2 or Scottish Levels A–B and C–E. It can be used as a flexible resource with any scheme, to fulfil National Curriculum and Scottish 5–14 requirements and to provide children with a variety of different learning experiences that will lead to effective acquisition of skills and knowledge.

POETRY

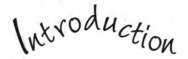

SCHOLASTIC CURRICULUM BANK POETRY

The *Scholastic Curriculum Bank English* books enable teachers to plan comprehensive and structured coverage of the primary English curriculum, and enable pupils to develop the required skills, knowledge and understanding through activities.

Each book covers one key stage. There are six books for Key Stage 1/Scottish levels A–B and six for Key Stage 2/Scottish levels C–E. These books reflect the programme of study for English, so that there are titles on Reading, Writing, Speaking and listening, and Spelling and phonics. The titles on Poetry and Drama cover all four aspects of the programme of study in relation to these subjects.

Bank of activities

This book provides a bank of activities which are designed to broaden children's experience of poetry and enable them to develop their ability to listen effectively, to read with understanding and to write confidently using a range of poetic forms and techniques.

Lesson plans

Detailed lesson plans, under clear headings, are given for each activity and provide material for immediate implementation in the classroom. The structure for each activity is as follows.

Activity title box

The information contained in the box at the beginning of each activity outlines the following key aspects:

▲ *Activity title and learning objective.* For each activity, a clearly stated learning objective is given in bold italics. These learning objectives break down aspects of the programmes of study for English and the National Literacy Strategy for teaching into manageable, hierarchical teaching and learning chunks, and their purpose is to aid planning for progression. These objectives can easily be referenced to the National Curriculum and Scottish 5–14 requirements by using the overview grid on pages 13 to 16.

▲ *Class organization/Likely duration.* Icons ✝✝ and ⏰ signpost the suggested group sizes for each activity and the approximate amount of time required to complete it.

Previous skills/knowledge needed

Information is given here when it is necessary for the children to have acquired specific knowledge or skills prior to carrying out the activity.

Key background information

The information in this section outlines the areas of study covered by each activity and gives a general background to the particular topic or theme, outlining the basic skills that will be developed and the way in which the activity will address children's learning.

Preparation

Advice is given for those occasions when it is necessary for the teacher to prime the pupils for the activity or to prepare materials, or to set up a display or activity ahead of time.

Resources needed

All materials needed to carry out the activity are listed, so that the pupils or the teacher can gather them together easily before the beginning of the teaching session.

What to do

Easy-to-follow, step-by-step instructions are given for carrying out the activity, including (where appropriate) suggested questions for the teacher to ask pupils to help instigate discussion and stimulate investigation.

Suggestion(s) for extension/support

In these sections, ideas are given for ways of providing easy differentiation. Suggestions are provided as to ways in which each activity can be modified for less able or extended for more able children.

Assessment opportunities

Where appropriate, opportunities for ongoing teacher assessment of the children's work during or after a specific activity are highlighted.

Opportunities for IT

Where opportunities for IT present themselves, these are briefly outlined with reference to particularly suitable types of program. The chart on page 159 presents specific areas of IT covered in the activities, together with more detailed support on how to apply particular types of program. Selected lesson plans serve as models for other activities by providing more comprehensive guidance on the application of IT; these lesson plans are indicated by bold page numbers on the grid and the icon at the start of an activity.

Display/performance ideas

Where they are relevant and innovative, display ideas are incorporated into activity plans and illustrated with examples. For many poetry activities, a performance may be an appropriate outcome rather than (or as well as) a display. In these cases, a range of performance activities is suggested.

Reference to photocopiable sheets

Where activities include photocopiable activity sheets, small reproductions of these are included in the lesson plans together with guidance notes for their use and, where appropriate, suggested answers.

Assessment

Assessment of children's work on poetry includes specific assessment of reading, writing, and speaking and listening. Assessment of speaking and listening may be more subjective than assessment of reading and writing; but it is still important to make a careful assessment and keep records of attainment. Each activity includes suggestions for formative assessment, and some can be used for a more formal, summative assessment of progress.

Photocopiable sheets

Many of the activities are accompanied by photocopiable sheets. For some activities, the sheet is a resource which the teacher can use in various specific ways within the activity, in order to provide differentiation by task. Other sheets are used for recording, or for relatively open-ended tasks, in order to provide differentiation by outcome. The photocopiable sheets provide purposeful activities that are ideal for assessment and can be kept as records in pupils' portfolios of work.

Cross-curricular links

Cross-curricular links are identified on a simple grid which cross-references the particular areas of study in English to the programmes of study for other subjects in the curriculum, and where appropriate provides suggestions for activities (see page 160).

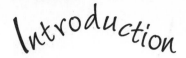

POETRY AT KEY STAGE 1

Poetry allows us to use language in exciting and imaginative ways. A poem can touch us, delight us and make us think. Even the youngest children respond eagerly to the rhymes and rhythms of poems, nursery rhymes and jingles.

Reading poetry aloud and listening to it can be a richly rewarding experience. Teachers should take time to explore and expand such reading sessions, choosing from a wide variety of authors, styles and cultures. Children should be encouraged to respond in a variety of ways to the listening experience. They may wish to talk about the poems, to question what they have heard, to draw or paint, or to present a dramatic response through role-play.

At Key Stage 1, children should be encouraged to follow poetic structures and patterns which allow them to substitute one word for another and to experiment with language. Such activities bring success and enable young children to view themselves, perhaps for the first time, as independent writers.

Young children also enjoy the experience of listening to poems, joining in the choruses and following the word patterns in books. Carefully-guided reading of both familiar and unfamiliar poetry texts will help children to focus on key words, rhymes and repetition. This work, in turn, leads towards successful independent reading.

A variety of well-illustrated poetry books should be made available to the children, so that they can find their own favourite poems and listen to the music of the language in their heads – even if they cannot yet read every word of the poem! The children should be led towards an appreciation of the pattern of the words on the page, and encouraged to discover new poems which they will enjoy reading for themselves.

Most children enjoy hearing old favourites time after time, especially poems that rhyme – just think of the enjoyment that nursery rhymes have given young children for generations. Children have a natural ear for rhythm and rhyme. They should be encouraged to listen to and recite poems with predictable and repeated patterns of rhyme.

It is generally accepted that the use of repeated rhymes helps children to develop reading skills. When they are listening to poems being read aloud, be ready to explore new rhymes with them and encourage them to see what happens to a poem when different rhyming words are substituted for the original.

Although young children enjoy the rhyming aspect of poetry, they should be introduced early to the idea that poems don't always have to rhyme. This is important, especially if children are experiencing difficulties with their own writing. There is nothing less desirable than the forced rhymes which children sometimes feel obliged to produce when they think that 'a poem must rhyme.'

Poetry is, above all, a way of playing with words. Children already have some experience of word-play through jokes, limericks, TV jingles and familiar playground chants; no child comes to school totally uninitiated into the music and language of poetry.

The Literacy Hour

The National Literacy Strategy suggests that better literacy standards are associated with a close connection between the teaching of reading and that of writing. The *Curriculum Bank Poetry* books (this book and the companion *Key Stage 2* book) highlight this principle. Each activity is designed to fit into a Literacy Hour, give or take ten minutes or so.

Most of the activities follow the procedure recommended in the National Literacy Strategy: some direct teaching input with the whole class, followed by grouped, paired or individual work and reading, writing and/or discussion concerning the content of the lesson.

Many of the activities are introduced through shared text work – either listening to poems being read aloud by the teacher, or class reading and discussion. In many cases, it is suggested that the teacher incorporate some of the children's ideas into a piece of class writing on the board or flip chart. Such guided writing should be orchestrated by the teacher, who can perhaps use a poetry pattern as a model. Later, the class poem can be copied out and used in a 'Big Book' or anthology, so that the children can use it as part of the classroom reading resources.

Within the Literacy Hour, it is also recommended that the children be asked questions in order to probe and extend their understanding. The activities in the *Curriculum Bank Poetry* books include open questions which will help children to reflect on what they have heard and read. They are encouraged to explore their ideas about published poems – and about the poets themselves.

The design of these activities creates ample opportunity to encourage discussion among the children, so that they can learn to evaluate their own and other children's work.

Where appropriate, it is suggested that the teacher stimulates and guides language exploration as recommended in the National Literacy Strategy.

In order to develop the children's writing, the books include many poems which provide structures, themes and ideas to which the children are invited to respond; they can use these poems as patterns for their own creative work. These patterns should first be modelled by the teacher from the children's suggestions, then used as a basis for independent writing. If some children are not yet ready to take part in independent writing, they should be given support in the form of guided text work with the teacher or another sympathetic adult.

Finally, at the end of the Literacy Hour, it should be possible for many of the children to share their finished work with others in the class. Production and display of 'best' work, in handwritten or word-processed form, are also encouraged, as is the use of role-play or performance to bring a further dimension to the children's written work.

Listening to poems

Poetry is for sharing, and the most effective way of sharing is to read poems aloud to groups of children or to the class as a whole. Listening sessions should take place in a comfortable carpeted area where there is little chance of being interrupted. They should be as varied, interesting and exciting as possible, and the children should be encouraged to take an active part.

Active listening involves questioning, discussing, choosing and making judgements about the poems. One way of encouraging this is to tell the children, before the

reading begins, that there will be a 'thinking time' when the poem is finished. This means giving the children a minute or so to think over what they have heard, perhaps using the time to make a picture of the poem inside their heads. Suggest that they think about new or special words, remember rhymes they liked or consider what might have happened after the poem ended. The children might also be encouraged to ask themselves questions about the way the poem has been written, or to think about the rhythms and sounds of the words themselves.

The listening and exploring sessions in these activities will often be followed by looking at the pattern the poem makes on the page. To make this part of the activity successful, all the children must be able to follow the words; so it is a good idea to enlarge the text, either by using the photocopier or by copying the poem onto an overhead projector transparency.

During this session, try to make sure that the children have some understanding of the connection between words *said* and words *read*. They should understand that print on the page is a series of symbols which allows us to read back words which have been spoken. They should also become aware of the arrangement of words to form lines (including repetitive features such as choral lines). This is an appropriate point at which to teach or reinforce the meaning of *word, line, verse, rhyme* and *title,* and to consider *capital letter, full stop* and so on.

In regular listening and reading sessions, the teacher should introduce a range of poetic styles: rhyming and non-rhyming poems, narrative and descriptive poems, long and short poems, and poems to make the children laugh out loud.

Children love playing with language. In this way, they learn what language can do – in speech, in stories and in poems and songs. Listening to the ways in which different poets make language work for them helps children to develop their own language abilities, and to deepen and extend their own vocabularies.

Children as writers

Poetry is an ideal way of practising the process of writing. It helps both the child and the adult writer to express thoughts and feelings directly. It is an economical way of writing: the poetic form encourages us to make every word work for its place.

In activities meant for the early stages of Key Stage 1, the children are often invited to substitute a single word or phrase, so that the revised poem has the child's own individual stamp and can be seen as a marker on the road to independent writing. For example, in 'Days of the week' (page 71), the children are asked to change one word in a highly predictable pattern. Working towards success in this way inspires confidence in even the most diffident young writer.

Children with learning difficulties can also be enthusiastic about writing poetry. A poem need not be long, and can be a lot of fun to write. Following a simple repetitive pattern usually brings success!

Teaching strategies

The following strategies are worth keeping in mind when teaching children to write poetry.

Listing

One of the most effective ways of using teacher input in the early stages of teaching poetry-writing is to concentrate on making a 'shopping list' of ideas. This can be done by asking the children for suggestions and scribing their responses (on a board or flip chart) in a simple list form.

It is a good idea to divide the list into sets of related words – for example, when working on an image poem about the sun, first collect ideas for toys (*balloon, frisbee, ball...*), then for food (*doughnut, orange, lemon lolly...*) and finally for flowers (*buttercup, sunflower, primrose...*).

Teachers often use a 'brainstorming' method to accommodate and organise all the ideas suggested by the children; but at Key Stage 1, the 'shopping list' method makes it much easier for young children to read and choose the words they want to use from the sets of ideas scribed on the flip chart.

Word-trading

When acting as scribe for the children, you should avoid the easy option of writing down the first things they say. Rather, you should 'trade words' with the children orally, building vocabulary word on word until there is a 'stack' of language available to them. For example, when describing the movement of a snail, the children can be encouraged to work from *'crawling'* to *'slithering'*, *'sliding'*, *'trailing'*, *'creeping'*, *'tracking'* and so on, using the opportunity to explore the richness of our language.

Following a listing and word-trading session, you can include many of the children's suggestions in a class poem. Using a specific pattern or structure, you can demonstrate how a poem is constructed – word by word or line by line. This process helps to give children confidence in their own ability to write a similar poem.

Patterns and structures

It is a mistake to assume that the use of a formal pattern will always inhibit the children's imagination. There is nothing more inhibiting, for either a child or an adult writer, than to be presented with a blank piece of paper and asked to write a poem on 'Spring' (for example) with no guiding framework. Working to the discipline of a strict poetry format, on the other hand, often releases the children to concentrate on images, descriptions and comparisons. Poems are a way of fitting words into patterns, and the children will be stimulated by the excitement of making words and ideas fit together like a jigsaw.

Drafting and editing

Shared and guided writing helps children to view drafting and editing as an important element in composition. Using published poems as models, show how words or phrases can be substituted to revise a poem and give it a new identity. Let the children take part as you work on the drafting process, and show them how a knowledge of phonic and sight vocabulary helps with accurate spelling.

As you begin the final editing process on the board, try

to explain how you are making your choices: looking for the most striking image or the most unusual word, looking at punctuation, making sure the rhymes work and checking on the rhythm. When the children have watched the teacher at work, it gives them confidence that they can do it too, and that crossings-out and rewrites are acceptable at the drafting stage.

Even when the children are first trying out their new-found writing skills, they can start to develop the habit of editing their own work. Encourage them to think about correct spelling. Perhaps the simplest approach is to make a practice of using individual 'word dictionaries', in which you write the words an individual child decides he or she needs. Encourage them first to look for the 'key' or initial sound, so that they have an initial input into the task of editing.

Encourage the children to devise their own 'shopping lists', so that they can make choices about the best words to use. Provide them with 'drafting books', and explain that these should be used like the flip chart – as a place to draft or try out a piece of writing. Remind them that they can cross out an idea if a better one occurs to them. A good drafting strategy is to underline any words that they are not sure how to spell, so that later they can consult a class or individual dictionary. Thus the flow of composition is not interrupted. If you correct a child's spelling, it is good practice to show how the *whole* word should look.

Teachers are often concerned about how much help children should be offered at the drafting stage, and this can be a major problem of organization – especially in the Key Stage 1 classroom, where a queue can form at the drop of a paper clip! The following strategies will help to minimize the demands made on teacher time:

▲ Encourage the children to review and revise their own work from the earliest days. Give them strategies to help with accurate spelling (see above).

▲ When working on drafting with individual children, look for no more than two points – for example, finding a better word and help with a spelling error.

▲ Working in groups and pairs can sometimes help children with the drafting process. They can either work with friends or in mixed-ability pairs or groups, with an independent writer encouraging one who is less confident.

▲ If there is a common problem, discuss it with the class. *'Can we all think how to help Sophie? She is trying to think of a white flower that the moon is like...'* You can then list some white flowers as suggested by the children, and Sophie can choose the one that best fits her poem; the list will also be helpful to other children.

▲ Be sure to say what part of a child's poem you really like. It will give the child a further boost if you read that passage aloud to the others – especially if the child lacks confidence in his or her writing ability.

Children who are used to working through the drafting

process do not regard the teacher's input as 'marking'. They want their work to look good at the next stage, when it is displayed in 'best' on the wall; and they look forward to presenting their poems as attractively as possible.

Presentation and performance
Imaginative displays of children's work are an everyday feature of most infant schools. When arranged with care and attention to detail, attractive displays demonstrate to the children that their work is valued by the adults in their world.

There are many interesting ways of displaying children's poetry: in one-poem books, zigzag books, flap-books, mobiles and so on. Class displays of children's work on a backing frieze can be shown alongside table displays of related books, pictures and artefacts. Vary the methods used for display – for example, encourage the children sometimes to use the word processor instead of handwriting (this is particularly useful for those children who are still developing hand control). The poems can be illustrated using paints, collage materials, felt-tipped pens, wax crayons or coloured pencils.

When the children have read, listened to and discussed poems, they should be given the opportunity to respond to them and present them through a range of drama activities. They will enjoy taking part in role-play and improvisation, often using minimal props such as hats and simple masks. They can enact the story of a narrative poem – for example, see 'The hardest thing in the world to do' (page 112) and 'The Secret Brother' (page 119).

The children should also be encouraged to present their own poems on cassette or to an audience. Some of their poems could be set to music – particularly rhyming poems or those with a lively beat. The children will enjoy giving a choral and musical performance in the style of a pop group.

Another performance option is the use of choral speaking. The poems presented could be the children's own, or ones from a published source. Choral speaking demands fairly rigorous practice, but the results can be very effective. Providing a musical backing, live or on cassette, will enhance the appeal of the performance.

The children should also be encouraged to learn to recite some poems and nursery rhymes by heart. This is a practice recommended in the National Literacy Strategy.

The imaginative leap

Although much of the written work at Key Stage 1 relies heavily on following a pattern or structure, there is always a place for the child who likes to chart his or her own course. When children demonstrate that they have the ability to take a 'sideways look' at everyday things, encourage them to use this gift. Children who are capable of taking an imaginative leap should be supported and encouraged. You should always be on the lookout for children whose work sends a shiver down the spine. They are the poets of the future!

Assessment

The best poetry surprises us with its unexpectedness – and this characteristic makes it very difficult to grade in terms of 'marks out of ten'. Assessment of children's poetry depends on knowing the children and the level at which they are capable of working. The teacher's personal reaction to the 'feel' of the poem is also crucial.

However, there are some questions that the teacher can consider when assessing a child's poem:
▲ Has the writer made the best and most surprising choice of words?
▲ Did the poem make you think again about its theme?
▲ Is the grammar correct?
▲ Is the punctuation correct?
▲ Does the rhyme or rhythm scheme work?
▲ Does every word of the poem count?
▲ How does the writer feel about the poem?
▲ Do other members of the class appreciate it?
▲ Did it give you a 'shiver down the spine'?
Children's responses to poetry read aloud are even more difficult to assess, but there are questions you can keep in mind:
▲ Does the child listen with interest and concentration?

▲ Can he or she answer simple factual questions about the poem?
▲ Is he or she able to explore, develop and explain ideas about the content of the poem?
▲ Does he or she understand the meanings of simple poetry terms such as *verse, line* and *rhyme*?
▲ Is the child sensitive to the feelings expressed in the poem?
▲ Can he or she predict 'what might happen next'?
▲ Can the child share ideas and insights with others in the class or group?
▲ Is the child eager to take part in a further poetry listening session?
▲ Can he or she make choices, and express reasons for liking or disliking a particular poem?
▲ Does he or she want to hear a particular poem again?
▲ Can he or she remember and recite any poems by heart?
When children are at the stage of reading poems for themselves, consider the following questions:
▲ Do they read poems for pleasure?
▲ Can they use anthologies to find poems already known to them?
▲ Can they follow the pattern a poem makes on the page?
▲ Are they interested in reading a range of different poems, not just the most 'fun' ones?
▲ Can they 'get lost' in a poetry book?

Overview grid

Title	Learning objective	PoS/AO	Content	Type of activity	Page
Reading and sharing					
Weather sounds	To explore the sound patterns of weather words. To join in choral repetition with actions.	Speaking and listening 1a, d; 2a; 3b. Reading 1c, d; 2a, b. Writing 1b. Awareness of genre, Level A. *Knowledge about language, Level A.*	A listening activity based on a weather poem. The poem uses onomatopoeia, and the children are encouraged to join in with their own ideas.	Whole-class listening, shared reading and discussion.	18
Kate's skates	To explore rhymes orally by substituting words and phrases.	Speaking and listening 1a, c, d; 2a; 3b. Reading 1a, c, d; 2a, b, c. Writing 1b; 2a. *Knowledge about language, Level B.*	An oral activity which explores rhyme, and in which the children are invited to participate.	Whole-class listening and discussion; group reading and oral creative work; then whole-class oral creative work.	20
Number rhymes	To explore and learn some traditional nursery rhymes based on number. To use these structures to experiment with similar rhyming patterns. To create a shared composition.	Speaking and listening 1a, c, d; 2b; 3b. Reading 1a, c, d; 2b, c. Writing 1a, c; 2a, d; 3b. *Awareness of genre, Level A.*	Listening to traditional number rhymes. The children are introduced to a rhyming narrative poem, and learn to identify a few poetic terms.	Whole-class discussion; group oral creative work; whole-class shared writing; individual writing or drawing.	23
Food, glorious food!	To compare and contrast poems on the theme of food. To choose a favourite poem and express reasons for the choice.	Speaking and listening 1a, c, d; 2b; 3b. Reading 1c, d; 2a, b, c. *As above.*	The children compare and contrast several poems on the subject of food.	Whole-class listening, shared reading, discussion and oral creative work.	26
Breakfast boast	To listen appreciatively to a story poem and discuss it using appropriate terms (such as rhyme and verses). To show awareness of humour in a poem.	Speaking and listening 1a, c, d; 2b. Reading 1a, c, d; 2c. Writing 1b, c. *Listening in order to respond, Level A.*	The children are introduced to a rhyming narrative poem. They learn the meaning of a few poetic terms.	Whole-class listening, shared reading, discussion and oral creative work.	29
A small dragon	To listen to a narrative poem being read aloud. To show understanding of the poem by commenting on aspects such as the choice of words and the use of implication.	Speaking and listening 1a, c, d; 2b; 3b. Reading 1a, d; 2a, b, c. *As above.*	Looking at another narrative poem: one which does not use rhyme, but which employs an interesting and imaginative use of language.	Whole-class listening, shared reading, discussion, storytelling and shared creative writing.	32
The secret brother	To listen carefully to a narrative poem and explore the language used in it. To predict and discuss possible endings to the narrative.	Speaking and listening 1a, c, d; 2b; 3b. Reading 1a, c, d; 2a, b, c. Writing 2b; 3b. *As above.*	This listening activity encourages the children to predict and discuss a range of alternative endings.	Whole-class discussion, listening and shared reading; paired oral work on using a telephone and inventing signs or codes.	35
What nonsense!	To listen to and read nonsense poems, appreciating their humour. To identify and discuss patterns of rhythm, rhyme and sound in these poems.	Speaking and listening 1a, c, d; 2b; 3b. Reading 1a, d; 2a, b. *As above.*	Looking at some nonsense poems which encourage appreciation of patterns of rhythm and rhyme.	Whole-class listening, shared reading, discussion and oral creative work.	37

POETRY

Title	Learning objective	PoS/AO	Content	Type of activity	Page
One poet, four poems	To explore, compare and contrast four poems by the same author and to respond to them imaginatively.	Speaking and listening 1a, c, d; 2a, b. Reading 1a, c, d; 2a, b; 3b. *Listening in order to respond, Level B.*	This activity encourages children to explore in depth the work of one well-known children's poet.	Whole-class listening, shared reading, discussion, oral creative work and performance; group discussion (of an author's poems).	40
Sounds like this	To explore the different sound patterns made by a variety of simple onomatopoeic poems. To take part in a shared writing experience.	Speaking and listening 1a, c, d; 2a, b. Reading 1c, d; 2a, b, c. Writing 1a, c; 3d. Listening in order to respond, Level B. *Imaginative writing, Level B.*	The children are encouraged to explore the sound patterns in a range of poems, and to participate in a shared writing activity.	Whole-class listening, discussion and shared creative writing; individual reading and reflection. Whole-class reading/listening and discussion, then group and individual writing.	44
Writing poems					
The secret creature	To write a simple shared composition and use its structure to create individual poems.	Speaking and listening 1a, c; 2a, b; 3b. Reading 1a, d; 2b. Writing 1a, c; 2a; 3b. *Imaginative writing, Level B.*	The children are introduced to a simple but effective writing pattern.	Whole-class discussion and shared drafting; individual creative writing based on a pattern.	48
How many stars?	To create a list poem through shared composition. To use this poem as a model for independent writing.	Speaking and listening 1a, c; 2a, b; 3b. Reading 1a, d; 2a, b. Writing 1a, c; 2a, b; 3b. *As above.*	The children use the model provided as a basis for independent writing.	Whole-class discussion and shared drafting; individual creative writing based on a pattern.	51
The sun	To be introduced to the concept of image. To write image poems using a simple poetic structure.	Speaking and listening 1a, c; 2a, b. Reading 1a, c; 2a, b. Writing 1a, b, c; 2a, b. *As above.*	This activity introduces the children to the concept of image.	Whole-class discussion and shared drafting; individual creative writing based on a pattern.	55
Looking closely	To use description and imagery to write poems based on close observation of objects.	Speaking and listening 1a, c; 2a, b; 3b. Reading 1a, d; 2b. Writing 1a, c; 2a, b. *As above.*	This writing activity is based on close observation of a range of objects. The children are encouraged to use descriptive words and phrases.	Whole-class discussion; group practical investigation leading to shared drafting of a poem.	57
At the seaside	To develop the ability to recognize and use descriptive language through writing a list poem with a repetetive pattern.	Speaking and listening 1a, c; 2a, b; 3b. Reading 1a, c, d; 2b. Writing 1a, c; 2a, b. *As above.*	This activity encourages the use of descriptive writing, offering a simple pattern for the children to follow.	Whole-class discussion and shared drafting; individual creative writing based on a pattern.	59
Opposites	To write patterned poems based on the idea of contrast, using a range of descriptive vocabulary.	Speaking and listening 1a, c; 2a, b; 3a. Reading 1a, c, d; 2b; 3b. Writing 1a, c; 2a, b. *As above.*	This writing activity explores contrast, and encourages the use of descriptive language.	Whole-class discussion and shared drafting; individual creative writing based on a pattern.	62
Poems in colour	To write a group poem based on a listing technique. To compare this with a published poem on the same theme, looking at structure, language and rhyme.	Speaking and listening 1a, c, d; 2a, b; 3b. Reading 1a, c, d; 2b. Writing 1a, c; 2a, b. *As above.*	This shared writing activity is based on word-listing.	Whole-class discussion and shared drafting; individual creative writing based on a pattern; whole-class performance.	65

POETRY

Title	Learning objective	PoS/AO	Content	Type of activity	Page
Using a pattern					
Who lives here?	To use a simple, repetetive poem as a model for composing patterned poems by introducing new words.	Speaking and listening 1a, c, d; 2a, b. Reading 1a, c, d; 2a, b. Writing 1a, b, c; 2a, b; 3a. *Imaginative writing, Level B.*	This activity uses a simple question and answer model as a pattern for writing.	Whole-class listening and discussion; group reading; whole-class shared writing and performance.	68
Days of the week	To construct a simple sequential poem through shared composition, based on a published poem. To learn and recite a simple sequential poem.	Speaking and listening 1a, c, d; 2a, b; 3b. Reading 1a, c, d; 2a, b. Writing 1a, b; 2a, b; 3b. *As above.*	A published poem is used as a pattern for simple sequential poems, based on the days of the week.	Whole-class discussion, oral creative work, listening and shared writing; individual creative writing based on a pattern.	71
In one second	To use a repetitive poetry pattern, substituting their own ideas for parts of the original poem. To read their own poem aloud.	Speaking and listening 1a, c, d; 2a, b; 3b. Reading 1a, c, d; 2a, b. Writing 1a, b; 2a, b; 3b. *Reading aloud, Level A.*	This activity uses a repetitive pattern; the children are encouraged to substitute new words of their own.	Whole-class discussion; group practical investigation; whole-class listening, shared reading, shared drafting and performance; individual creative writing based on a pattern.	73
Five senses	To create a class poem based on the pattern of a published poem, carefully selecting descriptive language. To read their own poems aloud, and to compare them with the original poem.	Speaking and listening 1a, c; 2a, b. Reading 1a, c, d; 2a, b. Writing 1a, b; 2a, b; 3b. *Imaginative writing, Level B.*	The class work with the teacher to create a poem based on an original published piece.	Whole-class practical investigation, discussion, listening, shared reading and shared drafting; group creative writing based on a pattern.	76
Countdown	To create a rhyming poem using a published poem as a model.	Speaking and listening 1a, c, d; 2a, b. Reading 1a, c, d; 2a, b. Writing 1a, b; 2a, b; 3b. *As above.*	The children are asked to create a new version of a given rhyming poem.	Whole-class listening, shared reading, discussion and shared drafting; individual creative writing based on a pattern.	79
For the first time	To recognize a chorus in a poem. To write a poem with a chorus, using a simple poetry structure. To compare and contrast two poems on the same subject.	Speaking and listening 1a, c, d; 2a, b. Reading 1a, c, d; 2a, b. Writing 1a, b; 2a, b. *As above.*	This activity encourages the children to write a chorus poem, using a given structure.	Whole-class listening, discussion, shared drafting and performance; individual creative writing based on a pattern.	81
When the wind blows	To use a simple, repetitive poetry pattern to compose their own poems through substitution.	Speaking and listening 1a, c, d; 2a, b. Reading 1a, c, d; 2a, b, c. Writing 1a, b; 2a, b; 3b. *As above.*	Another repetitive poetry pattern is provided as a basis for the children's creative work.	Whole-class discussion, listening, shared reading, performance and shared drafting; individual creative writing based on a pattern.	84

Title	Learning objective	PoS/AO	Content	Type of activity	Page
My home	To write poems based on the structure of a humorous poem, paying particular attention to rhyme and rhythm.	Speaking and listening 1a, c, d; 2a, b. Reading 1a, c, d; 2a, b. Writing 1a, b; 2a, b; 3b. *As above.*	The children are invited to use rhyme and rhythm to create a new version of a published poem.	Whole-class listening, shared reading, discussion and shared drafting (incorporating individual oral or written creative work).	86
Playing with forms					
Acrostics	To recognize and use the acrostic form in simple poems.	Speaking and listening 1a, c; 2a, b; 3b. Reading 1a, c, d; 2a, b. Writing 1a, b; 2a, b, d; 3b. *Imaginative writing, Level B.*	This activity introduces the children to the acrostic form.	Whole-class discussion and shared writing; paired creative writing, and then individual creative writing, based on a given form.	90
ABC poems	To use the structure of the alphabet as a starting-point for writing a poem.	Speaking and listening 1a, c; 2a, b; 3b. Reading 1a, c, d; 2a, b, d. Writing 1a, b, c; 2a, b, d; 3b. *As above.*	The children are encouraged to use their knowledge of the alphabet to structure an alliterative poem.	Whole-class discussion and shared writing; group creative writing, and then individual creative writing, based on a given form.	93
Kennings	To recognize and write kennings, exploring their possibilities.	Speaking and listening 1a, c; 2a, b; 3b. Reading 1a, c, d; 2a, b. Writing 1a, b, c; 2a, b; 3b. *As above.*	This activity encourages the children to recognize kennings and to construct their own.	Whole-class discussion and shared writing; individual creative writing based on a given form; performance and discussion within groups.	96
Recipe for a sandcastle	To write a poem using the format of a recipe.	Speaking and listening 1a, c; 2a, b; 3a, b. Reading 1a, c; 2a, b, d. Writing 1a, b, c; 2a, b. *As above.*	The children are invited to use the recipe form as the basis of a poem.	Whole-class discussion and shared writing; individual creative writing based on a given form.	98
Shape poems	To explore, discuss and write shape poems, paying particular attention to word-choice and visual presentation. To select concrete poems for a class anthology.	Speaking and listening 1a, c; 2a, b. Reading 1a, d; 2b, d. Writing 1a, c; 2a, b, e; 3b. *As above.*	The children are asked to consider how the shape of words on the page can be used to enhance the content of a poem.	Whole-class discussion, shared reading and shared writing; individual creative writing based on a given form; paired reading and discussion.	101
Riddles	To appreciate riddles as a form of poetry and to write their own riddles.	Speaking and listening 1a, c; 2a, b, d. Reading 1a, c; 2a, b, d. Writing 1a, c; 2a, b. *As above.*	The children are encouraged to invent their own riddles, and to solve those written by others.	Whole-class listening, shared reading, discussion, performance and shared writing; paired creative writing based on a given form, leading to whole-class performance and discussion.	104

Entries given in italics refer to the Scottish 5–14 Guidelines for English Language.

Reading and sharing

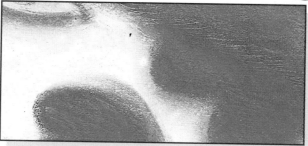

Poetry is meant to be shared. The most direct way of sharing poems in the Key Stage 1 classroom is for you to read aloud to a group of children sitting close together. Try to arrange that such a session takes place in the library or other comfortable area where books are displayed. Encourage them to listen with interest and courtesy. When you have finished reading the poem, allow the children a 'thinking time' of a few moments before discussion. Through open questions, explore with them the language used in the poems.

The reading and sharing session also offers teachers the opportunity to apply the National Literacy Strategy programme of objectives in shared and guided reading. It will be useful to enlarge the poems using a photocopier or OHP. Share ideas about the pattern the words make on the page, and explain the meaning of simple poetry terms such as *line, verse, rhyme* and *rhythm*.

The teaching of poetry is integral to the teaching of reading. Most poems are fairly brief, and they can provide a way of encouraging children to read books. Reluctant readers often appreciate the sound of the language used in rhyming and rhythmic poems. They can get caught up in the stories of narrative poems and enjoy the humour of funny poems. As well as listening to the teacher reading aloud, the children can follow the text and start to enjoy reading poems for themselves. They can use poems as stimuli for painting and drawing, act them out, learn them by heart or record them on cassette.

WEATHER SOUNDS

To explore the sound patterns of weather words.
To join in choral repetition with actions.

†† *Whole class.*
🕐 *30 minutes.*

Previous skills/knowledge needed

The children should be accustomed to listening to poems being read aloud, and be ready to join in reading aloud when invited to do so. They should know something about the different kinds of weather. They should also understand what it means to speak very quietly, and be able to raise the volume of their voices without shouting.

Key background information

This poem discussed in this activity relies on sound patterns and **onomatopoeia** – that is, using words whose sounds help to suggest their meaning. The poem builds up slowly to the sound of a storm, then gently dies away again. Use your voice to help children imitate this gradation when you invite them to join in.

Preparation

Make an enlarged (A3) copy or OHT of the poem on photocopiable page 108, so that all the children can read it together. You may find it useful to practise reading the poem aloud, so that you can use the required inflection. Obtain

some photographs and illustrations showing different kinds of weather. Use the classroom daily weather chart to record the week's weather.

Resources needed

Photographs and illustrations showing different kinds of weather, a daily weather chart, a board or flip chart, photocopiable page 108, writing materials (see 'Suggestion(s) for extension').

What to do

Gather the children together in a comfortable sitting area. Talk about what kind of weather you are having today: sunny, wet, cloudy and so on. Fill in the weather chart for that day. Show the children some pictures of different kinds of weather and discuss them. Can they say what clothes it would be appropriate to wear in the sun, the rain, the snow and so on?

Now ask the children to name the quietest kind of weather they can think of: something that makes no sound at all. They may suggest *sun, snow, fog, clouds*. If they go on to suggest a rainbow, take the opportunity to enlarge on this by explaining that rainbows usually appear after the rain stops; that it is difficult to see where a rainbow ends; and that according to legend, there is a pot of gold at the end of a rainbow. Go over the colours of the rainbow with the children: red, orange, yellow, green, blue, indigo, violet.

Now explore with the children the types of weather that make a noise: *rain, hailstones, wind, storm, thunder* and so on. Children often think that lightning is noisy; so explain that although thunder and lightning usually come together, it is thunder that makes the noise. Lightning makes the bright flashes that streak across the sky.

Tell the children you are going to read a poem about noisy weather. Suggest to them that the sounds of some of the words will help them to think about the kind of weather the poet is describing. Read the poem 'Weather is full of the Nicest Sounds' by Aileen Fisher aloud, using the inflection of your voice to indicate how the weather starts relatively quietly and then escalates, until you reach the lines *and mumbles / and grumbles / and rumbles / and flashes / and crashes.*

Ask the children whether they know what *grumbles and rumbles*, and what *flashes and crashes*. Talk a little about thunderstorms: the rain, the sound of the wind, the lightning flashes and the drumroll of thunder. If anyone is frightened of a thunderstorm, let them talk through their feelings. Find out whether anyone hides under the bedclothes or in the cupboard under the stairs. Explain that there is no real cause for them to be frightened if they are inside the house.

Tell the children that you need help to make the thunder sound really loud. Repeat the poem from *and mumbles...*, encouraging the children to join in, their voices getting louder as they move towards *and crashes*. They should

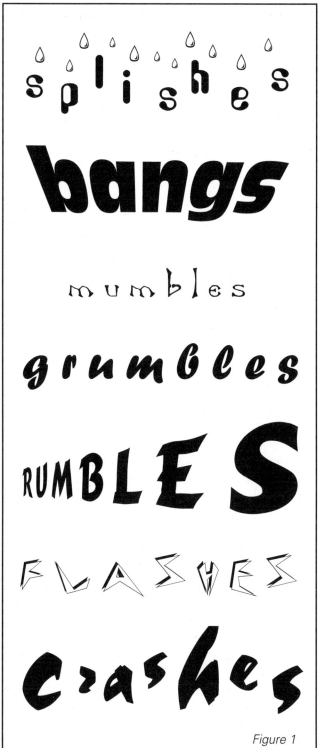

Figure 1

make a flashing movement with their hands for the lightning. Repeat this part again, making sure that the children use their voices to suggest the thunder (but without shouting).

Now read out the rest of the poem, making a wave shape with your hand when you get to the words *or a fish in the sea* and an emphatic *Not me!* (pointing to yourself) when you get to the end. Ask the children whether they can think of any creatures that might be frightened in a thunderstorm.

Where might they choose to hide?

Put up the enlarged version of the poem and read it through with the children. Go back to explore the weather words used at the beginning of the poem. Ask the children what kind of weather they think *sings / and rustles*. What other sounds might a gentle breeze make as it blows through the trees? Get the children to suggest new lines based on their own ideas – for example, *Weather is full / of the nicest sounds: / it whispers / and tickles / and breathes...* Go through a similar process with rainy sounds: *It drips / and drops / and bounces / and skips...* Make a list of new sound words on the flip chart.

Explore the rhyming words used in Aileen Fisher's poem: *mumbles, grumbles, rumbles...* Ask the children to think of more rhymes (for example *tumbles, fumbles, stumbles*). Find more rhyming words to go with *flashes and crashes* (for example, *bashes* and *dashes*). Look at the rhymes in the last verse: *bee, tree, sea...* See how many more rhymes the children can find to go with 'bee'. Keep this part of the activity purely oral.

Read the poem aloud again, getting the children to join in the lines they have rehearsed. They should go from quiet to loud, using their voices to make a comparison between the sound of quiet weather and the mighty sound of thunder. They should go quiet again towards the end, joining in with the actions and finishing with a confident *Not me!*

Suggestion(s) for extension

The more able children can copy out the first three lines of the poem, and then choose some weather-sound words from the flip chart (or make up new ones of their own) to invent a 'copycat' version of the poem, ending with the lines: *and flashes / and crashes*. They should read their new versions aloud to the others, and vary their voices to indicate the changes in the weather.

More able children could read the poem independently, or even learn part of it by heart.

Suggestion(s) for support

Children who need support can work with a more able partner. The pair can read together from the enlarged version of the poem, with the more able child giving confidence to his or her partner. Together (working orally), they can find three new weather-sound words to substitute for *pounds, twangs* and *bangs*.

Assessment opportunities

Note those children who enjoy the weather-sound words and invent new ones. Look for those who join in the repeated lines and use appropriate actions.

Opportunities for IT

You could create a word-processed file of the poem 'Weather is full of the Nicest Sounds', so that the children

can load it into the word processor and then experiment with different fonts, styles and colours to mimic the different sounds made by the weather. They will need to know how to highlight or mark single words or letters using the mouse. Once they have done this, they can change the font or font size (perhaps one letter at a time), alter the style (to **bold** or *italic*) and change the colour by selecting different colours from the options or menus. Figure 1 shows some examples.

Display ideas
The children can make free-standing zigzag books, showing a different kind of weather in each section. They can use paints, felt-tipped pens or collage materials for different effects – for example, autumn leaves glued on at random to suggest stormy weather, tissue paper for snowflakes, a painted rainbow, shiny paper scraps for raindrops.

Performance ideas
This activity lends itself well to dance and movement. To the sound of an adult (or an accomplished child reader) reading the poem, the children can make up an accompaniment with percussion instruments. They should follow the sound-words in the poem, exaggerating the actions of the wind, the raindrops, the thunder and so on to create a weather dance.

Reference to photocopiable sheet
The poem on photocopiable page 108 should be enlarged and used as a class 'Big Book' or OHT for pointing out sound-patterns and rhyming words.

A poem of sounds

Weather is full of the Nicest Sounds

Weather is full
of the nicest sounds:
it sings
and rustles
and pings
and pounds
and hums
and tinkles
and strums
and twangs
and whishes
and sprinkles
and splishes
and bangs
and mumbles
and grumbles
and rumbles
and flashes
and crashes.

I wonder
if thunder
frightens a bee,
a mouse in her house,
a bird in a tree?
A bear
or a hare
or a fish in the sea?

Not me!

by Aileen Fisher

KATE'S SKATES

To explore rhymes orally by substituting words and phrases.

†† *Whole class, then groups of 4 or 5.*
⏱ *30 minutes.*

Previous skills/knowledge needed
The children should know some familiar nursery rhymes by heart. It will be helpful if they know some other rhyming words, but this is not essential. They should be used to taking part in whole-class activities, and be ready to put forward their own ideas and suggestions.

Key background information
It is generally agreed that there is a correlation between children's appreciation of rhyme and their readiness to read. They should be helped to look for rhymes to use in their poems. Encourage them to concentrate on the fun element of rhyming: their new poems don't need to be perfect, just easy on the ear! This is purely an oral activity, with no writing required.

Preparation
Make an enlarged (A3) copy or OHT of photocopiable page 109. Photocopy a few familiar nursery rhymes from books. For those children who need support, make up a set of cards by photocopying page 110 onto card and cutting it into single pictures.

Resources needed
Photocopied nursery rhymes, books containing nursery rhymes, photocopiable pages 109 and 110, a board or flip chart.

What to do
Get the children sitting together as a comfortable group. Ask them whether they can remember any nursery rhymes. Encourage one or two of the children to say them aloud, helping out if they forget or get a bit embarrassed.

Repeat the nursery rhymes that the children have chosen, leaving off the end-rhyme (the second of each pair of rhymed words) each time. Make this a game where the others join in with the rhyming words – for example:

Humpty Dumpty
sat on a wall.
Humpty Dumpty
had a great ... *fall!*

Now ask the children to suggest more words which rhyme with 'wall': *ball, tall, stall, all.* Suggest that they make up some new lines – for example: *Humpty Dumpty / bounced a blue ball. Humpty Dumpty / grew very tall. Humpty*

Dumpty / slipped on a snowball. Humpty Dumpty / hid in the hall.

Divide the children into groups. Give each group a photocopied nursery rhyme (or let them choose one from the books), going over the words with them if necessary. Help each group to find new end-rhymes – for example:

▲ *Mary, Mary ... grow ... sew, low, go, mow.*
▲ *Hush a bye baby ... treetop ... stop, drop, mop, shop.*
▲ *Little Jack Horner ... pie ... fly, high, sigh, try.*

Give the children five minutes and ask each group to invent a new rhyming line – it can be as funny, silly or unlikely as they like. Applaud to show the children that you appreciate their efforts. (Should they come up with an unsavoury image, this may be a good opportunity to talk about 'appropriate language'.)

Settle the children down and tell them that you have a new rhyme for them. Ask if they know what 'Easy peasy!' means and when they might be likely to say it. Read the poem on page 109 aloud.

Let them reflect for a few seconds; then ask whether they know the name of the girl in the poem. Every hand should go up. Scribe *Kate* on the flip chart, and ask the children for rhyming words from the poem. Make a list of these: *Kate, skate, wait, eight, great, straight, plate, state.* Encourage the children to think of more – for example, *mate, delicate, ate, date, gate, late, chocolate, portrait, weight.*

Read out the first two lines of the poem again. Encourage the children to use substitution in the second line, making up new rhyming lines (as they did with the nursery rhymes). For example:

▲ 'I'll soon be eight, I'll soon be eight...'
▲ 'I won't be late! I won't be late!...'
▲ 'I'll climb the gate, I'll climb the gate...'
▲ 'I'll paint a portrait, paint a portrait...'

Now ask the children to suggest other easily rhymed names – for example, Ben, Sam, Clive, May, Polly or James. Ask them for appropriate rhyming words, and scribe these under the appropriate names on the flip chart – for example:

▲ *Ben... ten, then, men;*
▲ *Sam... lamb, ham, jam;*
▲ *Clive... dive, five, alive;*
▲ *May.... play, today, stay;*
▲ *Polly... dolly, jolly, Molly;*
▲ *James... games, flames, names.*

Using one of the new names, make up a new first line which follows the pattern of the original poem – for example: *'Easy peasy! Easy peasy!' said Ben...* Let the children come in with new rhyming lines, such as *I can count to ten* or *I can chase a hen.* Try again with other names, perhaps using the names of some children in the class. Make this a quick-fire oral game to be enjoyed by all of the children. Make sure that everyone has a turn, and be ready to help those who need support.

Finish the activity by rereading the original poem aloud

from the enlarged version, pointing to the words as you go along. Encourage the children to join in.

Suggestion(s) for extension

Let the more experienced readers work on a rhyming poem which follows the original pattern, but begins with another colloquial phrase such as 'Brill!' or 'Wicked!' (or whatever phrase is currently prevalent). Invent a scenario for the rhyme, such as a school, castle, playground or shopping centre. Help the children to collect an appropriate 'cast' for the poem, using easily rhymed words. For a castle poem, they might suggest *king, queen, prince, ghost, cook, frog, page.* Next, they should list possible rhymes: *king... sing, bring, thing, string...; ghost... toast, most, roast, post...;* and so on. Now they can use some of these ideas to create simple rhyming couplets – for example:

Cool castle rhymes

'Dead cool! Dead cool!' said the king.
'I can sing! I can sing!'
'Dead cool! Dead cool!' said the queen.
'I can dream! I can dream!'
'Dead cool! Dead cool!' said the ghost.
'I like toast! I like toast!'
'Dead cool! Dead cool!' said the bat.
'I've got a hat! I've got a hat!'

Suggestion(s) for support

For children who are struggling to find words that rhyme, use picture cards copied from photocopiable page 110 (see 'Preparation'). The children have to find new rhymes for the pictures (for example, for the plate, they might suggest

slit — black card

← Pull poem through slits →

Figure 2

figure of eight; Kate landing, feet up, in the slush with her Mum looking on. The words that Kate and her Mum use (see 'Opportunities for IT') should be placed in speech bubbles and pasted onto the pictures. The three individual pictures should be attached (in the right order) to a long strip of card. Finally, the children should make a TV set outline from black card and pull the strip along as an adult reads the poem aloud (or three confident children read out a verse each).

Reference to photocopiable sheets
Photocopiable page 109 should be enlarged to A3 size (or copied onto an OHT) for use as a 'Big Book'. Photocopiable page 110 can be photocopied onto card and cut up to make a set of picture cards for use in a rhyming game (see 'Suggestion(s) for support').

'Kate' or 'skate'; for the bat, they might suggest 'cat', 'rat' or 'hat'. The pictures can be used as playing cards in a rhyming game: the first player to come up with a suitable rhyme collects the card. (This game may need adult supervision!)

Assessment opportunities
Note those children who can find new rhyming words, and can then use them appropriately.

Opportunities for IT
The children could word-process the poem 'Easy Peasy' and any poems written by the class. These could be presented in large text to form a part of a 'Big Book' class anthology.

You could set up some template files with speech bubbles which have text boxes inside them. This can be done with a word processor which has graphics capabilities (Word for Windows has 'callouts' in the drawing tools which contain ready-made speech bubbles), or with a drawing package. Speech bubbles can often be taken from clip art collections and then enlarged or altered to fit the text. The children could then type in the words spoken by Kate and her mum in each verse:

Course I can skate...

Display/performance ideas
The children can make this poem into a 'TV spectacular', as shown in Figure 2. They need to make three large pictures or collages, depicting each of the verses of the poem: Kate skating with great confidence; Kate doing her

NUMBER RHYMES

To explore and learn some traditional nursery rhymes based on number. To use these structures to experiment with similar rhyming patterns. To create a shared composition.

†† *Whole class, groups, then individual work.*
🕐 *40 minutes.*

Previous skills/knowledge needed

The children should be able to read, write and order numbers to 10 (see the Programme of Study for Mathematics). They should be used to listening, and be ready to exchange ideas and take part in discussion. They should be able to identify 'families' of rhyming words and have some experience of playing with rhyming patterns.

Key background information

This is a simple rhyming activity based on traditional number rhymes, a few of which are suggested in the text. Any others can be substituted – perhaps ones specific to a particular region or an unusual method of counting (for example, *Mena, deena, deina, duss...*). Some of the rhymes may be new to the children. If so, take time to teach them – nursery rhymes are part of their literary heritage. In this activity, the children are encouraged to make up their own rhyming couplets. Don't be too concerned if they don't make a lot of sense: many traditional rhymes are so lost in the mists of time that they sound like nonsense to us as well!

Preparation

Make one copy per child of photocopiable page 111. Provide a variety of nursery rhyme books. Collect some examples of number rhymes, either published or written down from an oral source.

Resources needed

Photocopiable page 111, counting wall ladders or number lines, nursery rhyme books, number rhymes (see 'Preparation'), a board or flip chart, writing materials.

What to do

Gather the children in the story corner. Use a number line or wall ladder to point out the sequence 1, 2, 3, 4, 5. Go over this sequence with the children, then add the line: *Once I caught a fish alive.* Go on to *6, 7, 8, 9, 10 / Then I let it go again.* Ask whether anyone knows what happened next. Tell the children how the rhyme ends: *Why did you let it go? / Because it bit my finger so. / Which finger did it bite? / This little finger on the right.* Repeat the entire rhyme, encouraging the children to mime catching a fish, letting it go, then holding up and shaking the little finger of the right hand – obviously very painful!

Divide the class into two groups to perform the rhyme as a question and answer sequence. Repeat with the groups swapping lines. This helps the children to learn the rhyme by heart.

Introduce another counting rhyme: *One, two, three, four / Jenny at the cottage door / Five, six, seven, eight / Eating cherries off a plate.* Now adapt it, using names from the class and a new location: *Deema at the schoolhouse door...* If the children make an unworkable suggestion such as *at the front door,* use your voice to show them that a single beat doesn't fit. Explore orally some words that could make the line work: *at the new front door, at the red front door, at the glass front door.* Now experiment with the last two lines: *Five, six, seven, eight / Eating currants off a plate.*

Divide the class into two groups again and let them make up a new rhyme using some of their own ideas – for example:

One, two, three, four,
Darren at our neighbour's door.
Five, six, seven, eight,
Playing badminton with Kate.

One, two, three, four.
There goes Sally at our door.
Five, six, seven, eight,
Hurry up or you'll be late!

The children will enjoy the fun of this activity and be willing to go on for a long time, but five to ten minutes is probably enough!

Introduce another number rhyme: 'One, two, buckle my shoe'. Find out whether any of the children know what comes next, and teach the rhyme as you go. If necessary, use the number line to help the less confident children. Practise the rhyme with the whole class; then divide the class into groups, pointing to each group in turn to recite the next part of the poem. When you are satisfied that the children are familiar with the original, encourage them to create and substitute their own rhyming lines. They need to start by working on 'rhyme families':

POETRY

▲ *shoe, blue, do, stew, threw, drew...*
▲ *door, floor, pour, store, more...*
▲ *sticks, bricks, mix, tricks, fix...*
▲ *straight, late, plate, wait, mate, skate...*
▲ *hen, pen, men, then, den, garden...*

If appropriate, scribe some of the rhyme families on the flip chart. Where the children are not yet ready to read back the words, work orally with them.

Choose words from the family of rhymes to create a new version of 'One, two, buckle my shoe', encouraging the children to make suggestions. Help them to get the rhythm right by adding or deleting words as necessary. Once you and the children are happy with the new version, scribe it on the flip chart so that later on, it can be copied on a word processor and added to a class floor book anthology. The new rhyme might look like this:

> One, two, what shall we do?
> Three, four, lie on the floor.
> Five, six, carry some bricks.
> Seven, eight, cakes on my plate.
> Nine, ten, I've lost my pen!

Give out copies of photocopiable page 111. Ask the children to write a rhyming word (or draw an appropriate picture) alongside each pair of numbers.

Suggestion(s) for extension

More able children may like to learn the class poem by heart and recite it to the rest of the class.

Independent writers could use 'rhyme families' to create a long thin number poem – for example:

> One, fun
> Two, blue
>   Three, tree
>   Four, floor
>   Five, dive
>   Six, mix
>   Seven, heaven
>   Eight, gate
>   Nine, line
>   Ten, men

Suggestion(s) for support

With adult help, less confident children could learn some of the number rhymes by heart, exploring the rhyming words and perhaps suggesting substitutions. Photocopiable page 111 could be used by pairs for a simple rhyming game: each child draws pictures, and a partner has to identify the rhyming words.

Assessment opportunities

Note those children who can find and use appropriate rhyming words easily.

Opportunities for IT

Some children could copy out their number rhymes and format them in large print to add to the class anthology. Others could be encouraged to originate their work on a word processor. You could reduce the typing time by setting up a poem frame which includes the numbers. The children can then concentrate on drafting their ideas for the poem.

Some simple word processors allow the teacher to set up word banks. These could include a list of common

Figure 3

rhyming words for the children to choose from: they only have to select a word, and it is added to their line of the poem. Younger writers could be helped by an adult scribe typing their ideas. The discussion can thus focus on the most suitable ideas for rhymes.

Independent writers will enjoy creating a long, thin poem by spacing the couplets appropriately. They could be introduced to the use of the Tab key to move text along a line, instead of using the Space bar.

Display ideas

The children can make an illustrated wall-rhyme of 'One, two, buckle my shoe', using large numerals patterned in wax crayon or felt-tipped pen and cut out. Pairs of numbers can be stuck collage-style in a random pattern above the words – several 1s and 2s above the words *Buckle my shoe*, and so on. (See Figure 3.) Alternatively, an illustrated wall-rhyme could be made for 'One, two, three, four, five / Once I caught a fish alive' or any other number rhyme.

Performance ideas

The children can take part in a nursery rhyme extravaganza, perhaps dressing up for the part and reciting the nursery rhymes for parents and other relatives. This makes a welcome activity for Book Week, especially with very young children.

Reference to photocopiable sheet

Photocopiable page 111 is a writing frame with pairs of numerals, beside which the children can fill in appropriate

rhyming words or draw pictures to suggest rhymes. Less confident children can use the sheet for a rhyming game: each child draws pictures, and a partner has to identify the rhyming words.

FOOD, GLORIOUS FOOD!

To compare and contrast poems on the theme of food. To choose a favourite poem and express reasons for the choice.

†† *Whole class.*

🕐 *50 minutes.*

⚠ *Food must be handled only under careful supervision; strict hygiene procedures must be observed. If food is to be eaten, be aware of any food allergies or dietary restrictions.*

Previous skills/knowledge needed

The children should be used to listening to stories and poems being read aloud. They should be ready to share opinions and listen to comments on what they have heard. It will be useful (but it is not essential) for them to have some experience of different styles of poetry: rhyming and non-rhyming poems, descriptive poems and poems that play with words. They should also know about different kinds of food, and have some idea of where these foods come from.

Key background information

Food is central to the lives of most young children, and they hold strong opinions on what they like and dislike. They know a lot about the look, smell and taste of different foods, and are experts on sweets, drinks, ice-creams and most fast foods! This activity looks at some ways in which poets have described food that they have enjoyed. This activity explores rhyme, description and word-play.

Preparation

Enlarge the food poems on photocopiable pages 112, 113 and 114. Make a collection of illustrated cookery books and pictures of fruits and vegetables. It may be possible to borrow suitable posters from your local greengrocer. Obtain some poetry collections and anthologies including poems about food – *A Packet of Poems* edited by Jill Bennett (OUP, 1986) will be particularly useful for this activity (see 'Suggestion(s) for extension'). Provide some samples of fresh fruit and vegetables (to be touched, smelt and perhaps tasted). It might be a good idea to practise reading the tongue-twister 'Breakfast for One' (see page 114) aloud before you start the activity!

Resources needed

Cookery books, food pictures or posters, photocopiable pages 112, 113 and 114, a board or flip chart, some fresh fruit and vegetables, poetry collections and anthologies (see above).

What to do

Have the children sitting comfortably together as a group, and ask them about their favourite foods. Take time to listen to the various answers, giving most of the children a chance to express an opinion on the merits of hot dogs versus burgers, apples versus kiwi fruit, ice-cream versus candyfloss and so on. Write 'I like' and 'I don't like' lists on the flip chart.

Tell the children that you are going to read two poems about foods that most children like, and that you want them to listen and think about the words and ideas used by the

two poets. Read 'The Cupboard' followed by 'The hardest thing in the world to do' from the enlarged version of photocopiable page 112, which should be displayed. After a thinking time of a few minutes, ask the children how the two poems are different.

The most obvious difference is that 'The Cupboard' rhymes and the other poem does not. Explore both poems to see whether the children can point out the contrast between the sentiment of the lines *And when I'm very good, my dear / As good as good can be...* and the much more pragmatic waiting, watching and anticipating in Michael Rosen's poem. Ask which seems to be the more 'old-fashioned' poem, and why. A child might point to the *grandmamma* with *a very slippery knee.* What might make her knee or lap feel slippery? (The material of an old-fashioned, satin-type dress.) Ask whether their own grannies are like the granny in 'The Cupboard'.

The children will have no difficulty in empathizing with the child at the end of the ice-cream queue – this is probably a very familiar scenario to them. Find out which appeals more to them: the way the jar of lollipops is not described at all, or the way that we can almost see and taste the dripping ice-cream. Which words in the ice-cream poem create this effect? Is it the last line? Read both poems again.

Now read out another two poems: 'Picnic-packaged' and 'Harvest Festival' (photocopiable page 113). After the usual thinking time, ask what is the same about these two poems. The children may say that they both rhyme and are both about fruit. Point out how the poems are structured: both poems have four-line verses, but there are no breaks in 'Harvest Festival'. Follow this by getting them to look for differences – for example, there are lots of different fruits in the harvest poem, but only one in the picnic poem. Also, 'Picnic-packaged' goes into where and when the banana was grown, emphasizing its journey, whereas 'Harvest Festival' lists many fruits and vegetables that are all in the same place – the Harvest Festival table.

Put the enlarged version of photocopiable page 113 up

where the children can follow the words. Encourage them to look at the way the author of 'Harvest Festival' has listed everything on the harvest table. Let them handle the fresh produce, exploring the shape, texture and smell; or look at the fruit and vegetable pictures together and identify some of the things the poet has described. (Children sometimes need help to identify fresh vegetables, being more used to seeing them as tinned or frozen products.)

Ask the children to think of other fruits and vegetables which the poet might have added to her list: raspberries, strawberries, pears, cherries, peppers, beetroot and so on. Encourage them to suggest words to describe these foods – for example: *sweet squashy strawberries, ripe red raspberries, shiny green peppers...* Make this a quick-fire oral exercise.

Look at the poem 'Picnic-packaged' in more detail. Ask the children why they think the poet might have chosen this title. Explore the idea of *unzipping its thick yellow coat.* How else might that have been put? – *peeling its yellow skin, unfastening its bright jumper* and so on. What does this poem say about where bananas are grown and how they get here? Encourage the children to think about other foods which come 'half-way round the world': tea, coffee, oranges, melons and so on.

Now display and read out the two poems that play with words: 'Cake for tea' and 'Breakfast for One' (photocopiable page 114). Suggest that both poems were written for fun. Ask the children whether they know where the pattern of 'Cake for tea' has been borrowed from. (The nursery rhyme 'Pat a cake, pat a cake'.) Read it again and get the children to do all the actions, from mixing and whisking to rubbing tummies.

Read out 'Breakfast for One' again, letting the children enjoy hearing how well you tackle this tongue-twister! Look at the words the poet has used to describe her toast, and the different ways that she has mixed them about for dramatic effect. Look at the last line and ask why the poet has added it. The children may suggest: *It finishes the poem. It rhymes. It's easy to say. Marmalade is what you*

put on toast... and so on.

Finish the activity by contrasting all the poems, their content and the way they are written. Look at the pattern each poem makes on the page. Which poem has the most unusual appearance? 'The hardest thing in the world to do' is written like a few lines of prose. Discuss where the children might find a very short prose piece: magazine advertisements, posters, newspaper announcements and so on. Unlike the other poems, 'The Cupboard' has a choral line. *What makes up the chorus? In which verse is the chorus different? How does the choral line in this verse match the other choral lines?* (Look at the rhyme.)

Find out which poem the children enjoy most, and discuss why this is so. Is it the use of rhyme, the pattern on the page, the images it evokes or the sound of the words? The children are likely to enjoy 'Breakfast for One' and vote it their favourite. Their reasons for this preference may include the tongue-twisting element, the way that the same words are used over and over again, the dramatic punchline, or even the fact that it makes them feel hungry.

Suggestion(s) for extension
Groups of independent readers could search through anthologies and poetry books to find other food-based poems. Ask them each to choose a favourite poem, giving reasons for their choice, and to practise reading their chosen poem aloud with other members of the class. They might work together to create a *Big Book of Food Poems* anthology.

Suggestion(s) for support
Children who need support could work with copies of the poems (photocopied from pages 112, 113 and 114).

A group could be given an enlarged copy of 'Picnic-packaged' cut into individual lines, and asked to put the lines in order by identifying the rhyming words. They could go on to try this with the other poems in this activity. Ask

them which poem is the most difficult to arrange, and why. They should respond that 'Breakfast for One' is the most difficult, because it does not change the sense of the poem in any way if most of the lines are placed in a different order. Ask them which poem they think would be easiest to learn by heart, and tease out their reasons. ('The Cupboard' because it has a regular rhyme scheme? 'Cake for tea' because it is like a nursery rhyme? 'The hardest thing in the world to do' because it is like a bit of a story?) Explore the answers with the children.

Assessment opportunities
Note those children who can appreciate the different poetic techniques used in the six food poems. Through discussion, identify those who can contrast and compare the poems on more than one level.

Opportunities for IT
The children could use a word processor to write, design and print out their 'I like' and 'I don't like' lists for display in the classroom. They could use an art package or clip art to illustrate the lists.

Display ideas
Enlarged copies of the poems can be displayed with illustrations, alongside a table display of cookery books. The children can make illustrated 'I like' and 'I don't like' lists and pin them above the table display.

Performance ideas
Let a group of children dress up in white paper hats like cooks and recite the poem 'Cake for tea' with appropriate actions. Another group could stand in a long queue, shuffling up to an 'ice-cream van' (a poster with an appropriate picture and list of prices will suffice) and then coming away from the van licking imaginary ice-cream cones. The last child could be left with nothing as the man puts out a sign saying 'Sorry, no ice-cream until tomorrow'. As this goes on, another group could give a choral reading or recital of the poem 'The hardest thing in the world to do'.

Reference to photocopiable sheets

Photocopiable pages 112, 113 and 114 each contain two poems about food. Each pair of poems can be displayed (using an enlarged copy or OHT) and compared in detail, bringing out various stylistic similarities and differences.

Food poems (1)

The Cupboard

I know a little cupboard,
With a teeny tiny key,
And there's a jar of Lollipops
For me, me, me.

It has a little shelf, my dear,
As dark as dark can be,
And there's a dish of Banbury Cakes
For me, me, me.

I have a small fat grandmamma,
With a very slippery knee,
And she's Keeper of the Cupboard,
With the key, key, key.

And when I'm very good, my dear,
As good as good can be,
There's Ban...

Food poems (2)

Picnic-packaged

I peel my bendy banana,
unzipping its thick yellow coat
and think of how far it has journeyed
across the seas on a boat.

Once it grew like a finger
on a giant's bunched-up hand,
high on a tree in the sunshine
in the fields of a faraway land.

I bite into the creamy-white flesh
of my picnic-packaged food –
after coming half-way round the world
I'm surprised it tastes so good!

by Moira Andrew

Harvest Festival

Cabbages, cauliflowers,
crisp, crunchy swedes,
peppers and parsnips
and melons with seeds;
Onions and mushrooms,
potatoes for chips,
tomatoes, bananas
and apples with pips;
...k beans and broad beans
...s in a tin,
...juicy

Food poems (3)

Cake for tea

Mix a cake,
    whisk a cake,
pop it in the tin!

Bake a cake,
    cool a cake,
please may I begin?

Cut a cake,
    slice a cake,
put it on the plate.

Pass a cake,
    share a cake,
do I have to wait?

Bite a cake,
    chew a cake,
eat up every crumb.

Empty plate,
    no more cake,
all down in my tum!

by Moira Andrew

Breakfast for One

Hot thick crusty buttery toast
Buttery toasty thick hot crust
Crusty buttery hot thick toast
Crusty thick hot toasty butter
Thick hot buttery crusty toast
Toasty buttery hot thick crust
Hot buttery thick crusty toast –

with marmalade is how I like it
most!

by Judith Nicholls

BREAKFAST BOAST

To listen appreciatively to a story poem and discuss it using appropriate terms (such as rhyme and verses). To show awareness of humour in a poem.

†† *Whole class.*

🕐 *40 minutes.*

Previous skills/knowledege needed

The children should be able to listen and respond to a poem being read aloud. They should be able to follow the plot of a simple narrative, and to anticipate some of the rhymes used in the poem. They should understand why a smoke alarm is important in the home.

Key background information

By offering a strong pattern of rhythm and rhyme, the poem 'Breakfast boast' offers the children an enjoyable listening experience. They should be aware of the fun and fantasy element in this poem, and be able to see how all these factors make the poem successful. The children's ability to recognize rhyming words, and to find new rhymes, is also an important component of this activity.

Preparation

Make some copies of photocopiable page 116 (see 'Suggestion(s) for support') and cut each one into line strips. Make an enlarged (A3) copy or OHT of photocopiable page 115. Collect some pictures and/or models of dragons.

Resources needed

Photocopiable pages 115 and 116, pictures and/or models of dragons, a flip chart; writing materials (see 'Suggestion(s) for extension'); A4 paper, glue, drawing materials (see 'Suggestion(s) for support').

What to do

Gather the children together, seated in the library or other carpeted area. Introduce the activity by asking who has a smoke alarm at home. (Most modern homes are fitted with one.) Ask whether they have ever heard it go off. Establish the reason why an alarm has to be so noisy: to wake people up if they are asleep, to make sure that everybody can get outside quickly in an emergency.

Set the scene for the poem by asking the children to imagine what would happen if a dragon were to set off their smoke alarm. How would it do this? Establish that dragons are supposed to breathe smoke and fire. Tell the children that you have a poem you want to read aloud, and that they should be ready to listen and follow the story of the poem in their heads. Read 'Breakfast boast' aloud all the way through. Let the children have a minute or two's thinking time when the reading is finished.

Put the enlarged poem up where all the children can

see it. Explore with them the way in which it is constructed. Tell them that each 'section' of the poem is called a **verse**. Then ask: *How many verses are there in the poem? How many lines are there in each verse?* Read the poem again.

Ask the children to consider the father's reaction in the first verse. Why did he dial *999 in his head*? He didn't know what had set the alarm off until he dashed downstairs, so he was imagining all sorts of disasters.

In the second verse, the father finds *just a wisp of pearly smoke / and a tiny scaly creature*. Ask the children to think about other 'tiny scaly creatures', such as a baby lizard or a small snake. What made this creature different from others? Look at the words used to describe its smoky breath: *a wisp of pearly smoke*. Explore with the children what image this line conveys. Could they find a different way of saying the same thing? For example, *a ribbon of white smoke, a twist of milky smoke*.

Let the children read the third verse or follow your finger tracing the words. Ask them how the little dragon was feeling. Encourage them to look for clues in the poem – how the dragon looked, what it said and so on. Look at the last two verses together. These finish off the story, with the little dragon finding an important job. Encourage the children to think about what it would be like to have a dragon helping with breakfast instead of an ordinary electric toaster or grill. They would be able to ask for lightly-done or well-done toast, instead of having to change the setting. Why do they think the family would want to 'boast' about their dragon? What does *boast* mean?

Now look at the poem again, this time concentrating on the rhyming words. Read a verse, stopping just before you get to the rhyme; ask the children to say the correct word.

How do they know what to say? The children may suggest that the end words 'match'. Tell them that this matching sound is called a **rhyme** (as in 'nursery rhyme').

Tell the children that the poet didn't need to use these particular rhymes: there are lots of other words that rhyme, but these words fitted the story. Encourage them to suggest some new rhymes: *worst/cursed ... first, burst; smoke/joke ... yolk, stroke; tears/ears ... fears, jeers, years; puff/enough ... stuff, rough, bluff; boast/toast ... most, roast;* and so on.

Make lists of rhymes on the flip chart. Look at the phonic/spelling element of these rhymes – for example, *puff, stuff* and *enough, rough* sound the same, but are spelled differently. Can the children find more words like this?

Finish off the activity by encouraging the children to think of other things which one could get a dragon to do: light the oven, help on Bonfire Night, send up a rescue flare, strip paint from walls... Read the poem again, encouraging the children to join in.

Suggestion(s) for extension

Ask more able children to read the poem again for themselves. Discuss with them what features make it definitely a poem – for example: the words are in lines, the lines make verses, there are some words that rhyme. Ask them to write it out as a story (in prose), leaving out all the things that make the original version a poem.

Suggestion(s) for support

Less able children can be led to see how the poem was put together through reconstructing it. Give each child a copy of photocopiable page 116, cut into strips. The children should first underline the rhyming words, then put the lines

in order (using the enlarged version as a guide). They can do this a verse at a time, showing where each verse begins and ends by outlining it in a different colour. Encourage them to say what they are doing, using terms such as 'line', 'verse' and 'rhyme'. When you have checked their work, let the children glue the strips on an A4 background and illustrate the reconstructed poem. With help from more able classmates, they may be able to read it aloud.

Assessment opportunities

Look for those children who appreciate the storyline and the humorous element in the poem. Note those who can suggest alternative rhymes.

Opportunities for IT

More confident children could use the word processor to reconstruct a prepared version of 'Breakfast boast' with the lines of each verse in the wrong order. The children can use the 'cut and paste' or 'drag and drop' technique to rearrange the lines. They could go on to format the poem with an unusual font or with text colours; they may even be able to add clip art pictures of dragons.

Children could also use an art package to create a dragon picture, experimenting with different colours or effects to make the fiery breath. Their pictures could be added to the poems; or the children could select one or two interesting lines from 'Breakfast boast' and add these to the picture. With careful planning, the whole poem could be recreated through a series of pictures. These could be displayed on the wall or bound to make a class story book of the poem.

Display ideas

The children can paint pictures of dragons involved in jobs around the house: making toast, lighting birthday candles on a cake, helping a parent with a soldering job (parent and dragon should both be shown wearing safety goggles) and so on. The dragon's fiery breath can be made from red, yellow and orange tissue or crêpe paper, glued on collage-style. These illustrations can be displayed alongside the original poem, under the title 'Job-seeking dragons'.

Performance ideas

The children can role-play the story of 'Breakfast boast' with different children playing the dad, the rest of the family and the dragon (wearing a mask). Act as narrator, or have a confident child reading the poem, while the action takes place.

Reference to photocopiable sheets

Photocopiable page 115 should be enlarged to A3 size, or copied onto an OHT, for display during the lesson. Copies of photocopiable page 116 should be cut into strips and given to children who need help with understanding how the poem is structured (see 'Suggestion(s) for support').

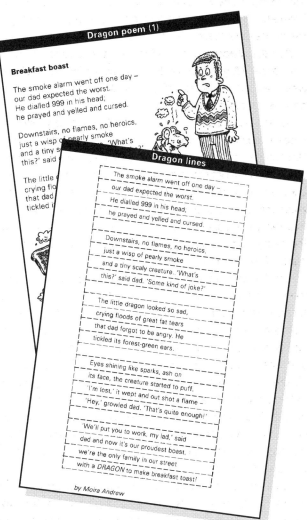

A SMALL DRAGON

To listen to a narrative poem being read aloud. To show understanding of the poem by commenting on aspects such as the choice of words and the use of implication.

†† *Whole class.*

🕐 *30 minutes.*

Previous skills/knowledge needed
The children need to be aware of the conventions of listening in a group situation: listening quietly, with concentration, ready to take turns to ask or answer questions. They should be familiar with dragons from legends or fairy stories.

Key background information
Dragons are found in stories and folk-tales from every culture in the world. They are said to be creatures of earth, air and fire: they crawl on the ground like lizards, fly like birds and breathe fire. The poem 'A Small Dragon' opens the children's imaginations to the 'What if?' aspect of finding a dragon in an ordinary place. Encourage them to suspend disbelief.

Preparation
Ask the children to bring in toy or model dragons from home: cuddly dragons, pottery dragons and dragons carved out of wood are all welcome. Collect some books, pictures and poems about dragons (see *Dragon Poems* edited by John Foster, OUP 1993). Make a 'Dragons' display. Make an enlarged (A3) copy or OHT of photocopiable page 117. Make some (A4) copies of photocopiable pages 117 and 118 (see 'Suggestion(s) for support').

Resources needed
Model dragons (see above), dragon-themed texts and pictures, a board or flip chart, photocopiable pages 117 and 118.

What to do
Gather the children together in the library or story corner. Initiate a discussion about dragons: *Has anyone ever seen a dragon? What do you think dragons look like? Where do*

they live? Does anyone know what a dragon's breath can do? and so on. Talk about a dragon's scales, wings, fiery breath; its cave, hoarded gold and so on.

Tell the children that you are going to read a story-poem about a very small dragon. Ask them to listen carefully, because you are going to ask some questions about the poem when you are finished. When everyone is settled and quiet, read aloud Brian Patten's 'A Small Dragon' (photocopiable page 117), bringing out the magic and mystery of the story.

Leave a 'thinking time' of a few minutes. Then suggest that everyone make a dragon picture inside their heads, using the poem. Go over the story with the group. *Where was the dragon found?* Talk about the things that are usually stored in a garden shed: rakes, forks, spades, bicycles and so on. Ask some of the children how they would feel if they found a dragon there. *Where might this dragon have been hiding?* (Under a flower pot, behind the spade, in the darkest corner.)

Ask the children whether they can remember where the dragon's real home was. If necessary, remind them of the line *Think it must have come from deep inside a forest.* Ask some more questions: *What colour was the dragon? What did the poet try to give it to eat? What happened then?* Ask the children to suggest food that might be used to tempt a frightened dragon. *Do you think the supermarket could be persuaded to stock cans of dragon food? What would the advert say? How would you advertise dragon food on TV?* From the children's ideas, scribe a dragon food slogan on the flip chart – for example, *Keep your dragon fierce and fiery with Hot Chilli Dragon Food!*

Now display the enlarged copy or OHT, and ask the children to concentrate on some of the details in the poem. *How big do you think the dragon is?* Most children will hold out cupped hands. Ask what clues the poem gives about the size – for example, *It made a nest among the coal / not unlike a bird's but larger...* Ask the children to say how the dragon's skin would feel (*damp*); explore with them other words which they might use to describe the feel of the small dragon. On the flip chart, scribe some of the feeling words the children suggest: *soggy, moist, cool like a frog, slimy* and so on.

POETRY

Ask about the colour of the dragon's eyes. The children may be able to interpret the line *leaves / are still reflecting in its eyes* as implying that the dragon has green eyes. Discuss the word 'reflecting'. *What else reflects shapes and colours?* (A mirror, a puddle, a lake, glass.) Ask them to look into a partner's eyes. *Can you see a reflection there? If so, what is it?*

Ask the children how they think the dragon might have been feeling. *What makes us think it was lost?* Re-read the lines: *it is out of place here / and is quite silent.* Can they think of other appropriate words to replace *quite silent?* They may suggest *lost and lonely, alone and sad, tearful and scared.* Explore with them the feelings that they may have had when they were lost in the supermarket, on the beach or in an unfamiliar street. (Now try stopping the tide of story-telling!)

Tell the children that there is a mystery at the end of this poem, because we don't really know what happens – the poet doesn't tell us. Read out the last verse again:

> If you believed in it I would come
> hurrying to your house to let you share my wonder,
> but I want to see
> if you yourself will pass this way.

Explore with the children the phrase *If you believed in it...* Ask whether anyone believes the poem is true. Talk about fairy tales and legends, and how stories about dragons are 'found' in all parts of the world (for example, in the tale of Saint George and the Dragon). Look at some of the dragon pictures that you have collected.

Ask the children why they think the poet says he wants someone *to share [his] wonder.* Perhaps it is because such a thing couldn't really happen; or perhaps it is because the small dragon was magical. Encourage a range of interpretations without insisting that any one is 'correct'.

Read the poem again, so that the children can enjoy a sense of familiarity with the story's events and the language used.

Suggestion(s) for extension

The more able children can explore further the language that Brian Patten uses, looking in particular at the ways in which he brings a sense of magic to his poem (for example, *I fed it on... / the roots of stars...*). Encourage the children to discuss (in a group) other ways in which the poet might have described the dragon's appearance – for example: *because its scales are spiky and green as grass... because it reflects sunlight in its eyes...* Suggest that they explore what the poet means when he says *it is out of place here.* What other words might he have used? (*It doesn't fit in here... It doesn't feel right here...*) Encourage the children to talk about times when they felt 'out of place' or not wanted.

The children should note the pattern of the poem: four verses of four lines each. Make the point that poems that do not rhyme can still have verses.

Suggestion(s) for support

Less able children could work with individual copies of photocopiable pages 117 and 118. They could start by colouring in the dragon picture, and highlighting the words in the text that tell what the dragon looks like. Using the empty space on the page, they could add pictures of a nest for the dragon to sleep in (*among the coal / not unlike a bird's but larger*) and the things it was given to eat. Ask them to name the foods in the poem.

Assessment opportunities

Look for those children who are absorbed by the narrative and the magical aspect of the poem. Note those who appreciate and understand the language used, and those who find it difficult.

Opportunities for IT

The children could work on screen with a prepared version of the poem 'A Small Dragon', highlighting specific words which describe how the dragon looks. The highlighting could be done by using different fonts, sizes, effects or colours. The completed versions could be printed out for display in the classroom.

The children could reconstruct a prepared version of the poem with the lines in the wrong order. Different versions

could have different parts or amounts of the poem in the wrong order. The children can use the 'cut and paste' or 'drag and drop' techniques to rearrange the lines. When they have completed the poem, they can format it with an unusual font or different text colours.

An alternative might be to create a large version in jumbo type, print it out, cut it into strips and then ask the children to reassemble it. The sorted poem can be pasted onto a large sheet to make a wall poem, or put into a class floor book anthology.

Display ideas
Draw the outline of a large dragon (perhaps by enlarging the illustration on photocopiable page 118). Ask the children to look for different shades of green in old magazine pictures or gardening magazines, and to cut them up into leaf shapes. They can then stick down the shapes like overlapping scales, working from the bottom of the picture upwards. (See Figure 4.)

Performance ideas
While the poem is being read aloud (by you or by an experienced child reader), four children can act out the story: one child looking for the dragon among the bits and pieces in the woodshed; another tempting it with new foods; a third looking puzzled as he or she walks away, followed by a sad-looking dragon (with a green dragon mask).

Reference to photocopiable sheets
The poem on photocopiable page 117 should be copied to A3 size or an OHT, for display during the lesson. The dragon

illustration on photocopiable page 118 can be coloured in and elaborated on to assist understanding of the poem (see 'Suggestion(s) for support'). An enlarged copy of this illustration can also be used as the basis of a display.

Dragon poem (2)

A Small Dragon

I've found a small dragon in the woodshed.
Think it must have come from deep inside a forest
because it's damp and green and leaves
are still reflecting in its eyes.

I fed it on many things, tried grass,
the roots of stars, hazel-nut and dandelion,
but it stared up at me as if to say, I need
food you c___ ___ ___ide.

A dragon picture

flames

overlapping scales in different shades of green

(Work from the bottom of the picture upwards.)

Figure 4

THE SECRET BROTHER

To listen carefully to a narrative poem and explore the language used in it. To predict and discuss possible endings to the narrative.

†† *Whole class, pairs.*

🕐 *40 minutes.*

⚠ *Use of the tin-can telephone should be carefully supervized to prevent accidents.*

Previous skills/knowledge needed

The children should be used to listening to poems and stories. They should be able to visualize a scene in their minds. They should be ready to suspend disbelief, so that they can accept the magic element in this poem.

Key background information

It is important to be aware that some children may have imaginary friends tucked away inside their heads, safe from their everyday lives, and may not want such fantasies to be exposed. If they are happy to talk about their own 'secret' friends, brothers or sisters, this is all well and good; but if there is any reluctance, try not to probe too much into their imaginative experiences, and concentrate instead on the story that Elizabeth Jennings tells. Encourage the children to think about why the poet (as a child) had to 'move Jack out', and to consider what might have become of him. Keep the discussion light.

When using the tin-can telephone, keep the string taut in order to carry the sound vibrations effectively.

Preparation

Construct a tin-can telephone from two cans and a length of string, as shown in Figure 5. (Also see *101 Science Surprises* by Roy Richards, Simon & Schuster Young Books 1992.) Make an enlarged (A3) copy or OHT of photocopiable page 119.

Resources needed

A tin-can telephone (see Figure 5), photocopiable page 119, a board or flip chart, drawing materials (see 'Suggestion(s) for support').

What to do

Seat the children in a comfortable area. Discuss with them ways in which we can pass messages to one another: letters, telephone, fax, e-mail and so on. Show the children the tin-can telephone, asking whether anyone knows what it is. Tell them that it is a very simple model telephone which will carry the sound of their voices along the string.

Let pairs of children try out the tin-can telephone, passing simple messages to one another across the classroom or hall. **NB** This will require careful supervision to avoid accidents with the string. Tell the children not to shout:

they should speak quietly and let the string do the work.

Settle the children down again and tell them that you are going to read a poem called 'The Secret Brother'. Remind them that there will be a thinking time at the end, and that they should use this time to go over the story of the poem silently inside their heads. Read out the poem and allow a few minutes for reflection.

Ask whether anyone can tell you about Jack. *Who was he? Where did he live? Who lived with him? What age was the poet when she was friends with Jack?* Establish, through questioning, that Jack lived with his old mother in

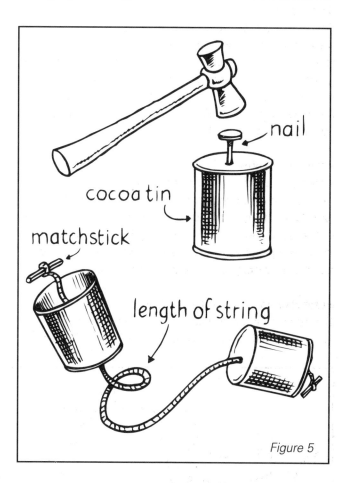

nail

cocoa tin

matchstick

length of string

Figure 5

the greenhouse at the bottom of the garden. Ask what the children think is odd about having a home in a greenhouse.

Show the children the enlarged copy of 'The Secret Brother' and read it aloud, pointing to each verse as you go along. In discussion, tease out the children's awareness that Jack wasn't real: he was an imaginary brother. Look for the lines that suggest Jack was a real person – for example, the opening lines (*Jack lived in the green-house / When I was six*) and the penultimate verse (*He and his old mother / Did a midnight flit*). Explain the meaning of 'midnight flit' if the children don't understand the phrase. Contrast these lines with the ones which indicate that he was only pretend – for example, *I didn't have a brother, / Jack became mine* and *Once my sister caught me, / Said "He isn't there...".*

Ask the children to think about what might have happened next (after the poem ends). Did Jack find another home? Did the child invent a new secret friend? If she did, where might he or she have lived? Or did the child grow out of imaginary friends? Discuss these and other possibilities with the children, sharing their experiences of secret friends if they wish to discuss these. If you had an imaginary friend in childhood, you might like to tell the children about him or her.

Explore with the children the magical, almost spooky element of the poem (for example, *Nobody could see him, / He never gave a sign*). Jack must have been invisible to everyone – perhaps even to the speaker. Ask the children to imagine what could happen if they had an invisible brother or friend. Encourage them to think of the games they could play and the tricks they could get up to. *No, Mum, I didn't leave muddy footprints on the kitchen floor. It was that Clare...*

Look together at the last verse, reading it aloud: *...And my brother making / Our own secret sign*. Get the children to think about signs people make: crossing their fingers, tapping their heads, raising their thumbs and so on. *What do these signs mean? What signs might Elizabeth and Jack have used?* Ask the children to work in pairs, inventing a secret sign and/or a secret code.

Bring the class back together. Ask the children to share their secret signs and codes. Record some of their ideas on the flip chart.

Suggestion(s) for extension

Organize the more able children into pairs. Let them work with the tin-can telephone, imagining what Jack and Elizabeth might have said to each other. They should bear in mind that the conversations took place at night: *With a tin telephone / Held beneath the sheet*. Let them report back to the class with their ideas.

The most able children might also be asked to make up a new final verse for the poem – for example:

Figure 6

Suggestion(s) for support

If some children have difficulty in making sense of the poem, work with them as a group, reading and discussing the poem two verses at a time. When you have finished working through the poem, and the children understand that the poem does not describe a real child, suggest that they draw a portrait of the 'secret' boy. Then help the children to invent a new title, such as 'My imaginary friend', 'Who lives in the garden?' or 'The invisible boy'. Scribe their suggestions on the flip chart, and ask the other children in the class to choose the one they think is the best.

Opportunities for IT

The children could work in eight groups, each copying a verse of the poem and then formatting it to fit on a page of a table-sized zigzag book. They could experiment with different font styles and sizes. They could also use an art

My brother and his mother
Never came back home.
I couldn't send a letter
And I didn't phone.

or Jack went away, but
He didn't go too far.
I saw him sail a moon-boat
And swing upon a star.

package to create their own pictures of what the 'secret brother' looked like. These could be added on screen to the word-processed verses; the pages could then be printed out to produce an illustrated zigzag book.

Display ideas

The children can use sugar paper or art paper to make a table-size zigzag book with eight pages. (See Figure 6.) When they have copied the text of Elizabeth Jennings' poem onto the word processor (see above) and printed it out, glue down the verses for them with one verse at the bottom of each page. Now ask the children to illustrate each verse, using paints, felt-tipped pens or coloured pencils. On the cover, put the title 'My Secret Brother' in bubble writing and add the poet's name. Use one of the children's portraits (see 'Suggestion(s) for support') to illustrate the cover. The book can be added to the poetry section of the classroom or school library.

Performance ideas

The children who have invented secret telephone conversations can use these as the basis of a class performance, speaking the lines they have made up and perhaps extending them.

Reference to photocopiable sheet

The poem on photocopiable page 119 should be enlarged to A3 size or copied onto an OHT for display during the lesson.

A mystery poem

The Secret Brother

Jack lived in the green-house
When I was six,
With glass and with tomato plants,
Not with slates and bricks.

I didn't have a brother,
Jack became mine.
Nobody could see him,
He never gave a sign.

Just beyond the rockery,
By the apple-tree,
Jack and his old mother lived,
Only for me.

With a tin telephone
Held beneath the sheet,
I would talk to Jack each night.
We would never meet.

Once my sister caught me,
Said, "He isn't there.
Down among the flower-pots
Cramm the gardener

Is the only person."
I said nothing, but
Let her go on talking,
Yet I moved Jack out.

He and his old mother
Did a midnight flit.
No one knew his number:
I had altered it.

Only I could see
The sagging washing-line
And my brother making
Our own secret sign.

by Elizabeth Jennings

WHAT NONSENSE!

To listen to and read nonsense poems, appreciating their humour. To identify and discuss patterns of rhythm, rhyme and sound in these poems.

†† *Whole class.*

🕐 *30 minutes.*

Previous skills/knowledge needed

The children should be accustomed to listening to poems and stories read aloud, and be prepared to exchange ideas and opinions. They should be able to recite the days of the week in order. For the second part of the activity, it would be helpful if they were familiar with the names of some common wild flowers (such as bluebell and foxglove); but this is not essential.

Key background information

This should be regarded as a light-hearted activity, though it is important to encourage the children to listen with care to the sound patterns and rhymes in the nonsense poems. The second part of the activity is more sophisticated, as it is a play on flower names: the children should be encouraged to think about the improbability of a fox 'putting on socks' – or, indeed, 'gloves'!

Preparation

Make enlarged (A3) copies or OHTs of photocopiable pages 120 and 121. It would be a good idea to practise reading some of the poems aloud – especially Michael Rosen's 'Say Please', which sets traps for the unwary tongue! Provide some books on wild flowers (for example, *Wild Flowers* by Richard Fitter and Marjorie Blamey, Collins 1985); and some anthologies of children's poetry (see 'Suggestion(s) for extension'), such as the *My First Poetry Book* series edited by John Foster (OUP).

Resources needed

Photocopiable pages 120 and 121, books on wild flowers, a board or flip chart, poetry anthologies, a weather chart.

What to do

Gather the children together in the listening corner. Ask whether they know what a 'tongue-twister' is. If they do, get them to try one out. Let the children listen to you reading aloud the 'Peter Piper' rhyme on photocopiable page 120. They will enjoy listening to your attempt to get through it! Tell them that 'Peter Piper' is a tongue-twister, and ask them to tell you why. *Because of all the Ps*, they may answer.

Now show the children the poem 'Say Please' by Michael Rosen (on photocopiable page 120), and ask them to listen to you reading it aloud. The second time, get the children to read it with you. This usually results in a lot of laughter and delight at the last two lines. Discuss why the poet might have opted for the doughnut. Replies may range from 'He likes doughnuts' or 'Fleas sandwiches aren't very nice' to the more thoughtful 'It's easier to say!' Ask the children to substitute a different ending: *I'll have a jam sandwich/a rice pudding/a mushroom pizza...* Encourage them to be inventive, while keeping to the structure of the poem. Scribe some of the new endings on the flip chart.

Read the poem again, asking the children to listen to the repeated rhyme: *please, cheese, knees, please, fleas...* It is a mixed-up poem – but what kind of sandwich did the poet want in the first place? *A cheese sandwich.* Encourage the children to look for more rhymes that would fit in this poem. They don't have to make sense (the children are unlikely to have eaten a knees sandwich) – but they do have to rhyme. They may suggest a *trees, breeze, peas* or *bees sandwich*; encourage unlikely, even ludicrous suggestions.

From the children's ideas, scribe a new 'Say Please' poem on the flip chart. The only rule is that it must keep to the same rhythm and rhyme as the original – for example:

I'll have a please sandwich cheese
No I mean a trees sandwich please
Sorry I mean a breeze sandwich please
No a please sandwich please
no   no –
I'll have a pepperoni pizza

Now ask the children to say the days of the week in order, using the weather chart if necessary. Tell them that you have some more nonsense poems for them! Read out 'Eataweek' by John Coldwell and 'Says of the Week' by John Foster (photocopiable page 121). Ask: *What do the words sound like?* The children should recognize that both poems are playing with the sounds of the days of the week. Discuss the way in which these poets are playing with words and sounds. Encourage the children to think of real words or invent nonsense words which sound like the days of the week – for example: *Monday/Funday, Tuesday/Bluesday, Wednesday/Bendsday, Thursday/Blursday, Friday/Sighday, Saturday/Latterday, Sunday/Noneday.* Scribe the best ideas on the flip chart.

Look at the enlarged version of 'Wild Flowers' by Colin West (photocopiable page 120) with the children. Explain that this is a different kind of nonsense poem: it is playing with the names of flowers by looking at them as if they were true. Look at a picture of a foxglove. Scribe the word and look at the way it is made up of two ordinary words: 'fox' and 'glove'. Ask the children to imagine what a fox would look like wearing gloves – or socks or shoes. They may remember the illustrations from *Fox in Socks* by Dr Seuss. Encourage them to suggest other items of clothing for the fox to wear: sunglasses, trainers, football boots...

Read out the first verse of 'Wild Flowers', and explore with the children the humour of the lines and the way in which the poet has played with the idea of a foxglove. Now look at pictures (in books) of the other wild flowers in the

poem: dandelions (with seed-bearing 'clocks') and bluebells. Read out the other two verses, encouraging the children to look at how the poet has treated the idea of a flower telling the time or ringing like a bell. Read the poem again, this time leaving off the rhymes and asking the children to supply the missing words.

Suggest that the children think of other words like foxglove and bluebell: words which are made up of two words put together, making something quite different. They may suggest other wild flower names (cowslip, buttercup) or insect names (butterfly, ladybird, dragonfly). Ask whether they think these words would be interesting to use in nonsense poems.

Conclude the activity by asking the children to say which of the nonsense poems they enjoyed most and why. Read all the poems again, encouraging the children to join in.

Suggestion(s) for extension

Children who are confident readers could look through some anthologies of poetry, collecting examples of nonsense poems. Ask them to practise reading these poems aloud, so that they can read them to the others in the class. They might make up a class book of nonsense poems, with a suitably zany title.

Suggestion(s) for support

Less confident children could work on 'Say Please' with a supportive adult, who could help them to find the rhyming words and substitute new ones. To make the poem different from the one scribed on the flip chart, change 'sandwich' to 'pizza'. Make this a fun activity, and ask the children to read their new poem aloud – for example:

Pizza please
Make me a please pizza cheese
no a pine trees pizza please
no I mean an anchovies pizza please
no   no –
I'll have some ice cream!

Assessment opportunities

Look for those children who can appreciate the nonsense element of the poems. Note which children can:
▲ supply new rhymes;
▲ identify the pattern of the poems;
▲ find interesting new 'double-words' which could be used as the basis of a word-play poem.

Opportunities for IT

Some children could use a word processor to copy their favourite nonsense poems (from the photocopiable pages or from other poetry books). They could experiment with different fonts and formats to enhance the poem's impact. The completed poems could be bound as a class anthology.

Display ideas

The children could make a large picture showing a fox wearing boxing gloves, a dandelion with a Big Ben-style

clock and a church with blue chiming bells. They could add illustrations of some other 'double-words'.

The children's 'Days of the week' poem (recorded on the flip chart) could be displayed in the form of an illustrated wall chart with the days as headings.

Michael Rosen's poem 'Say Please' could be used as the inspiration for a 3D display, showing a café in which chaos reigns. Price cards could declare 'Fresh Flea Sandwiches ALIVE only 95p', 'Try our NEW Knees Sandwiches NOW', 'Best Jam Doughnuts 20p each' and so on. The children can add their own ideas to the café counter.

Performance ideas

This activity lends itself well to end-of-term performances. Encourage the children to learn some of the nonsense poems by heart, so that they can take part in entertaining the audience.

Reference to photocopiable sheets

The nonsense poems on photocopiable pages 120 and 121 should be enlarged to A3 size or copied onto an OHT for display during the lesson.

ONE POET, FOUR POEMS

To explore, compare and contrast four poems by the same author and to respond to them imaginatively.

†† *Whole class, small groups.*

⏲ *50 minutes.*

Previous skills/knowledge needed

The children should be used to listening with concentration to poems read aloud. They should be prepared to share ideas and opinions about what they have heard, and be familiar with the courtesies of speaking and listening in a class/group situation.

Key background information

It is worth trying to familiarize yourself with Judith Nicholls' work. She writes poems and stories for children, using a range of styles and contexts. This activity encourages the children to listen with attention and imagination. It looks at the differences between strict rhymes and half-rhymes, as well as exploring a short non-rhyming poem. It also considers the magical element in much of this poet's work, contrasting this with her ability to write down-to-earth poems purely for the enjoyment of word-play. This activity reinforces some basic technical terms which the children need to discuss poetry: *verse, chorus, rhyme* and so on.

Preparation

Make enlarged (A3) copies or OHTs of photocopiable pages 122 and 123. Make one A4 copy per child of photocopiable page 123. Look for books containing more poems by Judith Nicholls, such as her collection *Storm's Eye* (OUP, 1994) or various contemporary anthologies of children's poetry. Obtain a photograph or picture of a spider's web.

Resources needed

Photocopiable pages 122 and 123, books containing more poems by Judith Nicholls (such as *Storm's Eye* by Judith Nicholls, OUP, 1994), a board or flip chart, a photograph or picture of a spider's web, writing materials (see 'Suggestion(s) for extension').

What to do

Gather the children in the story or library area, where they can sit together in comfort without being disturbed. Start by asking them what a person who writes poems is called. They may suggest *a poet, an author, a writer.* Ask them to explain the difference between these words. They may suggest: *A poet just writes poems. An author writes stories and poems. A writer does lots of different kinds of writing – poems, stories, newspapers, TV programmes...*

Explore with the children how they think a poet might go about working on a new poem. Talk about the stages of the writing process: thinking of an idea, drafting, editing and writing out in 'best' or typing. Relate this professional process to the way in which the children set about a writing task, and emphasize that they are basically the same.

Tell the children that there are four poems to read and listen to in this activity, and that the poems all have one thing in common: they were written by the poet Judith Nicholls.

Read the poem 'When?' (photocopiable page 122) aloud. Allow the usual thinking time, then put the enlarged version where it can be seen easily by everyone. Read it again, pointing to each line as you go along and encouraging the confident readers to join in. Encourage the children to comment on the pattern of this poem on the page; if necessary, remind them what a 'verse' is. Ask questions such as:

▲ *How many verses are there?* Three.
▲ *How many lines in each verse?* There will be some debate about whether the answer is three or four.
▲ *What about the fourth line?* It looks like a chorus – but it is different each time.
▲ *Do you notice anything about the first line in each verse?* It asks a question each time; only the first word is different.
▲ *How many questions and answers are there in this poem?* Five questions, three answers.

Ask the children to look for rhyming words. List them on the flip chart: *unfurled* (what does that mean?)/*world, track/back, brow/now.* Can they think of more rhyming words? They may suggest:

▲ *unfurled... curled, hurled;*
▲ *track... sack, black, stack;*
▲ *brow... bough, bow, how, cow.*

Ask them which word they think is the most difficult one to find rhymes for.

Ask the children to listen to the poem again, this time with their eyes closed. Afterwards, ask them to describe the magic horse in their own words. Explore with them the places to which the magic horse might go, and where they would like it to take them. Discuss the idea that this might be a dream poem, a wishing poem or a puzzle poem. Ask some open questions, such as: *Where might the horse have taken its rider? What did it eat? Where did it sleep?* Encourage imaginative responses.

Now look at the bottom of photocopiable page 122 and read the poem 'Magic' aloud. Ask the children what differences they can see between this poem and 'When?'. They may say: *It's much shorter. It doesn't rhyme. It hasn't got a pattern on the page.* The poem 'When?' was about magic; but this poem has the title 'Magic'. Ask the children to think about why this is. *What is the poem doing?* It is describing a spider's web, but the poet thinks it **looks** magical. *What was the weather like when the poem was written? What do you think the poet meant by 'glass beads'? Have you ever seen a spider's web after rain?*

POETRY

of night and day have their own rhythms. Discuss this idea in relation to other natural things within the children's experience, such as daisies opening and closing, blackbirds singing in the early light of morning, bats swooping in the summer dark and so on.

Direct the children's attention to the use of half-rhymes in this poem – for example, *song/dawn* and *June/gone*. Can they find any true rhymes? There are several, including *blow/below* and *white/light*. Look at the repetition of the line *There is no clock in the forest*. This poem can be called a 'circular poem', because it starts and ends in the same way.

Ask the children for their comments on this poem, comparing it – in terms of both content and style – with the other two that they have read during this lesson. Suggest that they try to make a picture of this poem in their heads. What colours would they be likely to use most? (See 'Display ideas'.)

Now, to show how much fun Judith Nicholls can have with words, give 'Sack race' (photocopiable page 123) a dramatic reading. Give out the individual copies of page 123 and read the poem a second time, encouraging the children to join in. When you judge that they are sufficiently familiar with the words, help them to recite the poem and perform the actions. Make this a very light-hearted part of the activity. It is noisy and causes immense hilarity, but is a useful counterpart to the long listening session. The children will particularly enjoy performing the final count as a rousing chorus.

Sit the children back down and suggest that they look for rhyming words. List these on the flip chart: *knees in/*

Show the children the photograph or picture of a spider's web. Ask them whether they can think of a different way of describing it. They may suggest *a lacy curtain, a mini-fishing net, Grandma's hair...* Ask them to describe the raindrops – *jewels, diamonds, glitter...* 'Magic' could be described as a 'snapshot' poem. It demonstrates that a poem can be very short and still be effective.

'Timeless' (see photocopiable page 123) is one of Judith Nicholls' best-known poems. Settle the children (if they have become restless) by doing some stretching, stand-up and sit-down exercises. Ask them to sit quietly and listen to a poem which combines a magical atmosphere with a description of a forest at night. Read 'Timeless' aloud. After the usual thinking time, ask whether anyone can suggest why the poet has called this poem 'Timeless'. Suggest that the poem answers that question in its first line: *There is no clock in the forest*.

Turn to the enlarged version of the poem and ask the children to read it with you, in soft mysterious voices. Ask: *What things in the forest take the place of everyday clocks and watches?* (A dandelion clock, the time when an owl hunts its prey, the song of the cuckoo...) Ask the children to explain how a dandelion clock works. Some of them may have tried blowing 'one o'clock, two o'clock' and so on. *Does it really tell the time?*

Ask what time of day it is when *an owl.... hunts / when the light has gone.* What time is *the bluebell light / of a day half-born / when the stars have gone*? It must be evening for the owl to go hunting, and dawn when the stars disappear. *Why does the poet say that there is no clock in the forest?* Help the children to see that there is no need for a mechanical clock, because the animals and the pattern

POETRY

squeeze in (discuss what is unusual about this rhyme), *knees/sneeze*, *hop/stop* and so on. Encourage the children to suggest more rhyming words which the poet might have used, such as *hold on/rolled on* or *flop/drop*.

To conclude the activity, organise the children into groups and ask them to discuss the four poems they have read and heard. (You may need to give them a quick reminder.) Encourage them to think about the different styles of the four poems, and the fact that these very different poems were all written by the same poet. After they have had some time for discussion, give them five minutes to choose the poem they liked best; then ask all the groups to report back to the whole class with their reasons.

Suggestion(s) for extension
Encourage the more confident children in this group to look through books to find more poems by Judith Nicholls, choosing the ones that interest them most. They can mark these with bookmarks and read some aloud to the other children later on. They might also like to copy some out in order to make a class anthology: *The Best of Judith Nicholls*.

Suggestion(s) for support
For children who require support, it may be better to concentrate on the two simplest poems: 'Magic' and 'Sack race'. Explore with them the contrast between the rhyming form of 'Sack race' and the non-rhyming form of 'Magic'. Encourage them to say what they like and dislike about each poem.

Assessment opportunities
Note those children who can listen with attention and imagination, those who can think about what might happen next, and those who can find new ways of describing things. Also look for children who are able to recognize differences in style between poems.

Opportunities for IT
The children could use an art package to create pictures of the forest at different times of the day. They could experiment with different colours, tints, shades and colour washes. They may need to be shown how to mix colours or to select different shades from a colour picker. With some art packages, it may be necessary to work in a multi-colour mode (256 colours or more) to provide a wide enough range of shades.

Alternatively, the children could use an outline starting picture on screen to create their own picture of a different time, season or atmosphere by adding effects. The starting picture could be drawn by the teacher or an older pupil, or scanned from another line drawing or even a suitable photograph (scanned in black and white mode). It should be saved to disk, so that the children can retrieve it, work on it and then save their versions under new file names.

The completed pictures could form a class display, or be added to a word-processed version of the poem 'Timeless'.

Display ideas
When the children are listening to and discussing the poem 'Timeless', they are asked to visualize the poem in their heads (see 'What to do'). The poem describes nightfall and early morning in the forest; so most of the colours would be black, grey and silver, with flashes of white or pale blue (*the thin white / of the early dawn* and *the bluebell light*). Encourage the children to turn their mental pictures into real artwork, using charcoal for the trees and bushes (concentrating on strong lines) and filling in other details more faintly with white chalk and a trace of blue in the sky. Their pictures can be displayed beside an enlarged version of the poem.

Reference to photocopiable sheets
The poems on photocopiable pages 122 and 123 should be enlarged to A3 size or copied onto an OHT for display during the lesson; A4 copies of page 123 should also be given to the children.

SOUNDS LIKE THIS

To explore the different sound patterns made by a variety of simple onomatopoeic poems. To take part in a shared writing experience.

†† *Whole class, then individual work.*

🕐 *40 minutes.*

Previous skills/knowledge needed

The children should be used to listening to poems and stories being read aloud and taking part in group discussion.

Key background information

This activity deals with sound patterns and onomatopoeia, and can be used as a follow-up to 'Weather sounds' (page 18). The children should be encouraged both to listen to the sounds around them and to think imaginatively about these sounds. The activity also helps children to make the connection between words said and words read, and gives practice in simple phonics. The shared writing task is a valuable way of encouraging co-operation between the teacher and children, and among the children themselves. In this activity, the writing task builds on reading and sharing; the activities in the next chapter deal specifically with children's writing.

Preparation

Make enlarged (A3) copies or OHTs of photocopiable pages 124 and 125. Collect some everyday things that make different noises: a pencil sharpener, a wind-up clock (with a loud tick), a hairdryer, a mixer (or other kitchen implement), beans or pebbles in a jar, car keys and so on. Find a large bag or box to hide the 'sounds' in.

Resources needed

Photocopiable pages 124 and 125, some 'noisy' objects (see above), a box or bag (in which to hide the objects), a board or flip chart; writing materials, marker pens (see 'Suggestion(s) for extension'); A4 paper (see 'Suggestion(s) for support').

What to do

Gather the children together in the library corner. Tell them that they are going to take part in a listening game – which means that they must use **their ears only**. Tell them that they have to cover their eyes and listen, then guess what is making the sound they hear. They should put up their hands when they know what the sound is, but they must **not** call out. Show them the bag or box of 'sounds'.

When the children are ready, take out one of the objects – for example, rattle the car keys. Ask for guesses. When you have shown them the keys and rattled them again, ask the children to say what kind of sound they make. Look for words such as *chinking, rattling* and *clicking*. Scribe the most evocative words on the flip chart.

Now do the same with the clock (for example). When the children have guessed what it is, look for words which describe the sound: *ticking, tocking, beating, pecking...* Encourage them to make up some words using appropriate sounds. Scribe some examples on the flip chart.

Follow this procedure for five or six different objects, then tell the children that you are going to read a poem which has lots of sounds in it. They should listen carefully and take a few minutes' thinking time before commenting on the poem. Read out 'Metal fettle' (photocopiable page 124). After a minute or two, ask whether anyone remembers a sound word from the poem (*clank, chink, tinkle* and so on). Display the poem and ask the children to read it aloud together. Discuss how the sound words help to bring the things described in the poem into their heads.

Encourage the children to choose some alternative sound words – for example: *The gurgle of a tank / the clatter of chains / the rattle of tins / the chugging of trains*. Repeat this oral exercise with the rest of the poem, trying to give every child the opportunity to suggest a word. If the first words suggested are inappropriate, explore other ideas until the group is satisfied. Spend about five minutes on this part of the activity.

Read the poem aloud again, this time concentrating on the rhymes. Pause at the end of the last line in each verse, and ask the children whether they can remember the correct word.

Now read aloud a second sound poem: 'Storm trouble' (see photocopiable page 125). Gather the sound words orally. They are also the rhyming words: *pops/drops, whirls/swirls, clashes/(flashes), thunders/blunders*. Ask whether anyone can say which word in this list does not describe a sound – the answer is *flashes*. Why do they think the poet has used it? Thoughtful answers might include *Thunder and lightning go together* and *To make it rhyme like the other words*.

Look for more storm words which might be substituted for those in the poem – for example: *rain drips, drops, plops; wind blows, flows, whistles; thunder bangs, crashes, explodes.* Let the children enjoy listening to the poem again, this time following the words on an enlarged photocopy or OHT.

Now read aloud the poem 'Kitchen sounds' (also on photocopiable page 124). When you have finished, ask the children to look at the enlarged version silently, searching for sound words. There are some unusual and exciting words in this poem: *gloops, sizzles, gurgles* and so on. Let the children hear the mixer, a whisk or some other kitchen implement. Ask them to find sound words to express the noise it makes: *whirr, buzz, whirl, churr...*

Encourage the children to explore other sounds which could be heard in the kitchen: the sounds of a food mixer, fridge, coffee percolator, frying pan, wok and so on. Then there are the things that we do: pouring juice, knocking out ice-cubes, opening a packet of biscuits, bringing potatoes to the boil... Ask the children to search for words to describe these sounds.

Construct a model poem on the flip chart, using some of the children's suggestions. Encourage them to use their knowledge of 'key' phonics to offer initial sounds. Scribe lines with two or three words each (as in 'Kitchen sounds') – for example:

Let the children offer more ideas. Suggest that they store these phrases inside their heads for later use in their writing. Discuss the common element in the three poems: sound words. Explain how the sound words match the movements made by the kitchen implements and machines.

Suggestion(s) for extension

Children who are independent writers could go on to create their own 'Kitchen sounds' poems, using any of the ideas which have been suggested or which they have thought of for themselves. Suggest that they follow the pattern on the flip chart, perhaps making up another four lines (or more). They could read their first drafts to the other children and elicit comments. Finally, they can write out their poems in 'best' inside kitchen utensil outlines drawn in marker pen (see 'Display ideas').

Suggestion(s) for support

If possible, arrange for a group of less confident children to work with a supportive adult. He or she should take the children's suggestions for a shared kitchen poem (as above), scribing the nouns in one colour and the verbs in another. The words can then be cut out and scrambled to make a nonsense poem like the following:

Pans spin,
the kettle pops,
potatoes crackle
and juice roars.

In the kitchen
Juice popples,
potatoes bubble,
cornflakes crackle,
biscuits crunch.
The fridge purrs,
washing rumbles,
the toaster pops,
the cleaner roars.

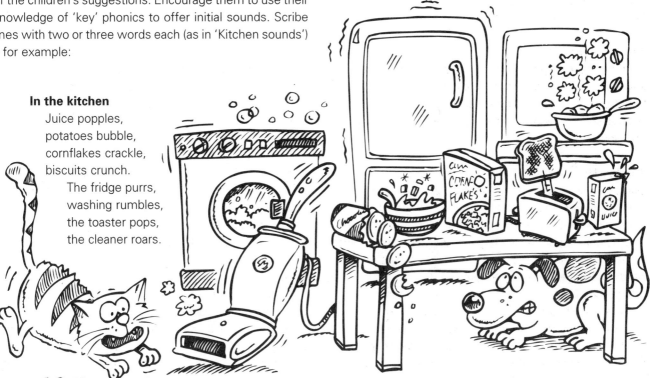

Figure 7

The children can read their nonsense poem aloud to the rest of the class.

Assessment opportunities

Note those children who can explore sound words and who can, in some cases, invent their own. Note also those who correctly use the plural or singular form (for example, *potatoes boil, an egg boils*). These observations can be based on the children's oral work, though any written work will provide further evidence.

Display ideas

The children's poems can be written inside kitchen utensil outlines (a pan, mixing bowl, kettle and so on), which can be pasted randomly on dark backing paper. This frieze can be given a title such as 'The noisy kitchen'. (See Figure 7.) A range of actual kitchen equipment and cookery books could be shown as a related table display.

Performance ideas

The poems on photocopiable pages 124 and 125 can be used as the basis of a performance for other children in the school. Ask the performers to learn a few lines by heart and to say them at the appropriate point in a group recital. They should exaggerate the sound words, bringing out the evocative sounds of *pops, gloops, sizzles* and so on. They may be able to use actions and sounds together to enhance their performance, perhaps using kitchen items as props.

Reference to photocopiable sheets

The poems on photocopiable pages 124 and 125 should be copied at A3 size or as OHTs for display to the class during the lesson.

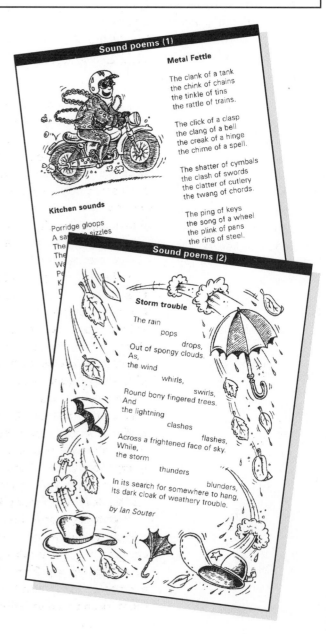

Writing poems

Writing a poem gives young children opportunities to develop their language skills in specific ways. The task of substituting one word for another requires children to search their vocabulary for synonyms. Through making 'shopping lists' and, later, through brainstorming, they learn to 'trade words' (or phrases) and to look for the most apt, unusual or satisfying word. Such methods lead children to deepen their knowledge of the language: its words and their power.

The teacher can help the children by using shared or guided writing techniques. At this stage, it is best to keep to a simple structure with a repetitive pattern. List some of the children's ideas on the flip chart and select the most interesting words and phrases. Demonstrate the early drafting process: crossing out, rearranging and so on. In this way, you can model many of the strategies which go into crafting a poem.

Help the children to understand that this process is involved in writing all poems: inspiration or listing, drafting, revising and presentation. This will give them the confidence and the tools to work on their own, going through the stages to the end result. Encourage them to play with language, to experiment with words, and to develop a feeling for rhythm and rhyme.

Eventually, some KS1 children will leave patterns and structures behind to pursue their own ideas. Young children have a fresh outlook that allows unusual poems to spring from the exploration of everyday encounters and mundane objects. Then the teacher must learn when to let go!

POETRY

THE SECRET CREATURE

***To write a simple shared composition and use its
structure to create individual poems.***

†† *Whole class, then individual work.*

🕐 *45 minutes.*

Previous skills/knowledge needed

The children should be accustomed to trading words and
sharing ideas in a class situation. They need to have a fairly
wide vocabulary. They should understand how adjectives,
verbs and nouns are used (though at this stage they do not
need to know these terms).

Key background information

This activity is based on a patterned and predictable
structure consisting of strings of adjectives, nouns and
verbs. The structure should first be modelled on the flip
chart or board from the children's suggestions, using the
'word-trading' method (see Introduction, page 10) to help
them explore appropriate language. Then the children follow
the pattern, using substitution to make up their own
versions of the poem. This should be a very exciting activity
for everyone involved. It works well with a topic such as
Minibeasts or Gardens.

Preparation

Make one copy per child of photocopiable page 126. Obtain
a small interesting-looking box with a lid and conceal a
dramatic-looking model of a small creature in it. (I use an
embroidered spider with waving legs!)

Resources needed

A box with a model creature (see 'Preparation'),
photocopiable page 126, a flip chart or board, marker pens
or chalks in four different colours, pencils, coloured pencils,
wax crayons (or felt-tipped pens).

What to do

Gather the children in the library or story area where they
are unlikely to be distracted. Make sure that the flip chart
or board can be seen easily by everyone.

Tell the children that you have brought a tiny visitor into
the classroom. Show them the box and tell them that a
very small creature lives inside. Discuss differences
between the little creature's 'house' and their own homes.
*It's smaller than my house. It's got coloured patterns. It's
got no doors and no windows. It's round.*

Tell the children that you want to write a poem about
the little creature – but the trouble is, he's very shy. Put the
box on a shelf and say that you will let them see inside it
later, when the little creature 'wakes up.' Tell them that
you are going to start with a guessing game, and ask them
to suggest creatures small enough to fit inside the box.
They will give you lots of ideas, from 'ant' to 'woodlouse'.
Give as many children as possible the opportunity to take
part.

When the children have run out of suggestions, say that
you are going to use some of their ideas to make a class
poem; but those whose creatures have not been used
should remember their ideas, as they will get the chance
to use them later on.

Turn to the flip chart and list five or six of the creatures
in the middle of the sheet. Use one colour for this list (for
example, red). Your list might look like this:

> snail
> caterpillar
> ladybird
> woodlouse
> beetle
> dragonfly

Keep flying creatures such as butterflies, dragonflies and
moths until last. Point out that you have used a red pen for
these names. Encourage the children to read through the
list with you. Now suggest that you are going to look for
words that describe how they imagine each creature might
look. Suggest that this is no ordinary creature: you don't
want ordinary brown snails and green caterpillars, but
something much more unusual! For example, you might
elicit *turquoise, lemon, swirly, patchwork* as 'describing
words' for a snail.

Spend a few minutes 'trading words', with the aim of
deepening and extending the children's descriptive
vocabulary. (See Introduction, page 10.) Then choose a word

that sounds unusual, or take a word suggested by one of the less confident children, for each creature. Using a different colour (for example, blue), add the adjectives to the left-hand side of the list. The result might look like this:

a crimson snail
a turquoise caterpillar
a luminous ladybird
a clockwork woodlouse
an indigo beetle
a patchwork dragonfly

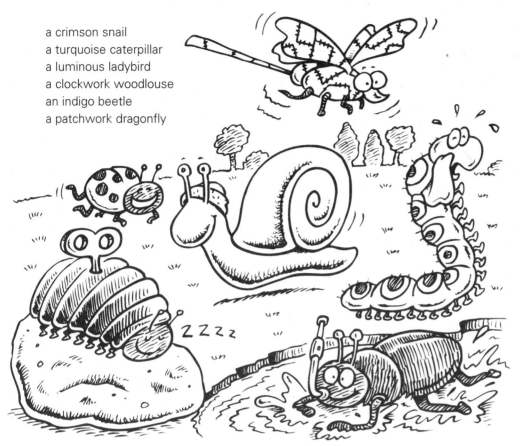

When you reach the flying creature (such as *dragonfly*) at the bottom of the list, encourage the children to explore a range of variations on the theme of 'flying'. You might elicit *floating, gliding, fluttering, hovering, soaring* and *rocketing*, ending your list with *a patchwork dragonfly floating.*

Tell the children that they have almost written a poem! It still has to be 'topped and tailed' with a suitable beginning and ending. Remind them that they should think of a suitable title for the poem. They may suggest *The mystery creature, The secret of the box* or *The unknown thing.* Choose a title from those offered and show how the simple question *Is it...?* beneath the title can link the various lines together. Then add a question mark to each line. This is a suitable opportunity to reinforce the children's understanding of what a question mark is and how it can be used.

Read this extended list with the children, making it clear how much you enjoy the exciting language. Reinforce the fact that the words in blue are describing words. Take time to discuss their meanings, and let the children relish the taste of new words on the tongue.

Now encourage the children to think of unusual doing words which say how the creature is moving or what it is doing. Hold up the box to remind them of the shy creature at the centre of their work. Tell them that all the doing words in this poem must end in 'ing'. Encourage them to think of 'way out' ideas – for example, they might suggest *gardening, swimming, jogging, rollerblading, trampolining...* Once the children have tuned in, their imaginative scope is infinite!

Using a different colour (for example, green), scribe doing words at the right-hand side of the list:

a crimson snail jogging
a turquoise caterpillar crying
a luminous ladybird laughing
a clockwork woodlouse sleeping
an indigo beetle swimming

To conclude the poem, ask whether anyone knows what kind of creature lives in the box. How can they find out? *Let's open the box. Let's look inside. Let's lift the lid... and look!* Take a suggestion as a closing line. The 'top' and 'tail' should be scribed in a new colour.

Let the children take pride in their shared writing by reading the poem aloud together:

The secret creature
Is it
a crimson snail jogging?
a turquoise caterpillar crying?
a luminous ladybird laughing?
a clockwork woodlouse sleeping?
an indigo beetle swimming?
a patchwork dragonfly floating?
Let's lift the lid and look!

Hand out copies of photocopiable page 126. Show the children how they can make up their own poem, following the pattern on the flip chart. Show them how to choose a describing word (blue), the name of a creature (red) and a doing word (green) for each line. Remind those children

whose original ideas were not used that their words should still be inside their heads, and that these ideas can be substituted for those on the flip chart. If the children have personal dictionaries, scribe any words that are unfamiliar to them into their dictionaries (if necessary).

If they wish, the children can rewrite their poems with new titles, tops and tails. They can use crayons or felt-tipped pens to decorate the edge of the poem with a variety of small creatures. When everyone has finished, let the children see the secret creature in the box. This is an exciting moment, and one which the children will thoroughly enjoy.

Suggestion(s) for extension
Encourage children who are independent writers to create their own poems, following the shared writing pattern but using a different scenario – for example, *Who is hiding in the tree? Who is hiding in the cave?* or *Who lives in the sea?*

> Who lives in the sea?
> Is it
> a silver squid diving?
> a golden starfish floating?
> a sunken ship rocking?
> a beautiful mermaid singing?
> Let's swim under the waves and see!

Suggestion(s) for support
For less confident children, ask a supportive adult to scribe a group poem from their suggestions. If the children are writing their own pieces, let them leave out the doing word, so that the poem might read: *Is it / a red beetle? / a blue butterfly? / a green spider? / a yellow wasp? / Let's look!*

Assessment opportunities
Look for those children who can use a wide vocabulary, and who enjoy the sense of power that creating a poem can bring. Note also those who can follow the structure given.

Opportunities for IT
Some children could use a word processor to draft their poems. To speed up the process, and to allow the children to concentrate on the creative aspect of their work, you could prepare a starting file with the structure and key words already entered. The children can then simply retrieve the file and work on the adjectives and verbs, as in the main activity. They should save their version under a different name, to make sure that the original file is not overwritten. The starting file might look something like this:

> **The secret creature**
> Is it
> a   snail
> a   caterpillar
> a   spider
> a   woodlouse
> Let's open the lid and look!

The children could even use different colours or font styles and effects to make their poem more exciting – for example:

> a   crimson   snail   **j o g g i n g**
> a   turquoise   caterpillar ***crying***

The children could also use an art package to draw their own creatures, which could be added on screen to the word-processed versions of their poems.

Display ideas
Paint a garden background with tall grasses and bushes, using different shades of green. Ask the children to design, colour and cut out some butterflies, snails, slugs, beetles, bees and so on, using bright patterns. Glue these cut-out minibeasts all around the grasses, keeping wings free so that they can 'fly' out of the picture. Put the children's poems around the frieze as a border. (See Figure 1.)

Reference to photocopiable sheet
Photocopiable page 126 provides a writing frame based on the 'secret creature' idea (rather than on any existing poem).

'free-flying' butterflies

children's poems

grasses in different shades of green

Figure 1

Encourage the children to write their own poems on this sheet, following the pattern on the flip chart and substituting new words where they can.

Sound poems (2)

Storm trouble

The rain
   pops
      drops,
Out of spongy clouds.
As,
the wind
      whirls,
            swirls,
Round bony fingered trees.
And
the lightning
      clashes
Across a frightened face of sky.
            flashes,
While,
the storm
      thunders
In its search for somewhere to hang,
            blunders,
Its dark cloak of weathery trouble.

by Ian Souter

HOW MANY STARS?

To create a list poem through shared composition. To use this poem as a model for independent writing.

🕐 *40 minutes.*

†† *Whole class, then individual work.*

Previous skills/knowledge needed

The children should have the ability to count up to ten, and should recognize the numerals 1–10. They should be able to share ideas orally and take part in class discussion. They should also be able to write independently, or at least to copy a simple pattern of words from the flip chart.

Key background information

This activity is characterised by initial oral work to which all the children should contribute. Their input should be encouraged, and their ideas extended wherever possible. You should be ready to provide a model poem based on the children's suggestions. This poem can be altered and amended as the session progresses. Let the children see that it is quite in order to change a poem while it is still at the drafting stage.

Preparation

Make one copy per child of photocopiable page 127, and some copies of photocopiable page 128 (see 'Suggestion(s)

Figure 2

stars or *10 shiny stars* or *10 bright stars*. Let them choose which adjective to add to the poem.

Now make a nine-star chart using a different colour, so that you have (for example) *9 silver stars*. Glue stars onto the remaining sections of the black backing sheet, going down to 2 stars and choosing a different star colour each time. Let the children either suggest words for the colour or find a different description for each group of stars.

Leave out 1 for the moment. Tell the children that you will look for something which is by itself in the night sky, and let them think about that idea – but ask them not to suggest anything.

Now encourage the children to explore words which say what stars do: *shining, glowing, twinkling, dancing, gleaming* and so on. Expand the list poem on the flip chart to accommodate these verbs, so that it looks like this:

10 golden stars shining
 9 silver stars exploding
 8 crimson stars twinkling
 7 yellow stars dancing...

Now add a title. Encourage the children to think about what the stars look like and suggest images. Scribe these to develop the poem:

for support'). Find some published number poems, so that the children can prepare their own anthology. *Number Poems* edited by John Foster (OUP, 1993) is a useful source. Pin up a large sheet of black paper, divided into ten sections, so that it can easily be seen by the children when they are sitting on the carpet.

Resources needed

Photocopiable pages 127 and 128, a number line to 10, star charts or photographs of the night sky, sticky-backed stars sorted into nine colours, one cut-out moon shape in white, black paper, a board or flip chart, writing materials.

What to do

Gather the children together in the library area. Look at some star charts or photographs of the night sky. Initiate a discussion about night and the stars – for example, exploring the idea that the stars are very far away. Talk about how astronomers use telescopes to find out more about the stars and space.

Let the children count out ten gold stars. Enlist their help in sticking them onto the first section of the sheet of black paper. (See Figure 2.) Ask the children about this 'star picture'. *Where do you think it might be?* (A night sky, the sky at Christmas, a shop window, fireworks...) *Can you find words to describe how the stars look?* (Golden, shiny, bright, like glitter...)

How many stars are there? Ask the children to count down from ten to one, using the number line if necessary. Tell them that you are going to write a countdown poem about stars. Scribe the first line on the flip chart, using an adjective which the children have suggested: *10 golden*

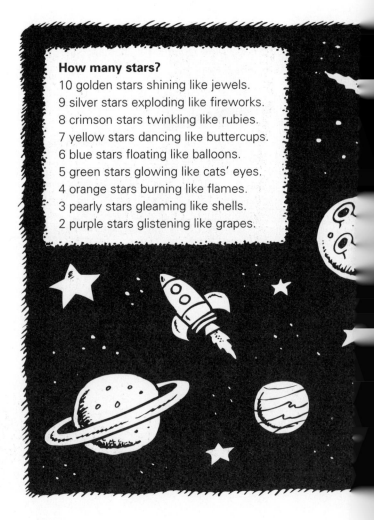

How many stars?
10 golden stars shining like jewels.
 9 silver stars exploding like fireworks.
 8 crimson stars twinkling like rubies.
 7 yellow stars dancing like buttercups.
 6 blue stars floating like balloons.
 5 green stars glowing like cats' eyes.
 4 orange stars burning like flames.
 3 pearly stars gleaming like shells.
 2 purple stars glistening like grapes.

And what is there only one of in the night sky? *The moon!* Explore with the children ways in which the poem might be finished off – for example, *1 milk-white moon sailing like a boat* or *speeding like a spaceship* or *curling like a fingernail...* Scribe the line which the children like best to complete the poem on the flip chart.

Give out copies of photocopiable page 127 and writing materials. Encourage the children to write their own version of the poem by substituting their own choice of words for the words on the flip chart. For example, they might write: *10 silver stars glowing / 9 red stars shining / 8 pearly stars gliding...* Those children who are ready to invent and write down images (similes) can be encouraged to do so.

Children who are keen to do so can read their finished poems aloud to the rest of the class. The children can also divide into groups to read out the poem from the flip chart, each group reading two lines.

Suggestion(s) for extension

Children who are confident and independent writers could work with you to create a rhyming list poem on the flip chart. Start by asking where the stars are shining: *in the night sky, in the sky at Christmas-time, in the dark...* Show how the first two lines can be extended to make a rhyming poem – for example, starting with *10 golden stars glittering*

in the night. Ask the children to find a rhyming word which goes with night: *fight, bright, white, might...* Encourage suggestions for a line which uses one of these words and fits into the general theme of the poem – for example, *9 silver stars shining very bright* or *9 pearly stars glowing milky-white.*

Go on to produce a group rhyming poem, such as the following:

> 10 golden stars glittering in the night.
> 9 silver stars shining very bright.
> 8 crimson stars twinkling in the dark.
> 7 yellow stars dancing across the park.
> 6 blue stars glowing in the sky.
> 5 green stars glistening way up high.
> 4 orange stars burning like a fire.
> 3 pearly stars singing like a choir.
> 2 purple stars gleaming from above.
> 1 milk-white moon flying like a dove.

This will demand a concentrated effort both from you and from the children; but it will extend the children's language skills considerably, and give the writers a real sense of satisfaction when the poem is completed.

Suggestion(s) for support

Children who need support with independent writing could work with the writing frame on photocopiable page 128. This is a more straightforward counting poem whose rhythm may remind the children of 'The twelve days of Christmas'. Help the children to build a list of appropriate things (such as *planets* and *Martians*), and scribe these on the flip chart using (for example) a red marker. Then make another list, using blue this time, with the children's suggestions for doing words. The children can now create their own number poems on the writing frame. For each line, they can choose a word from the red list, write it down and then add a word from the blue list. The resultant poem might look like this:

How many?
I flew into outer space one day.
Everything there came out to play.
There were
   Ten spacecraft spinning,
   Nine rockets flying,
   Eight comets burning,
   Seven Martians lurking,
   Six planets crashing,

   ... and so on.

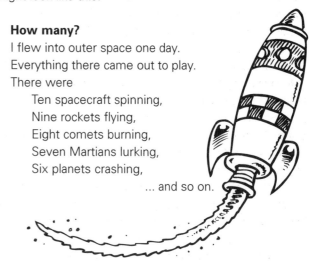

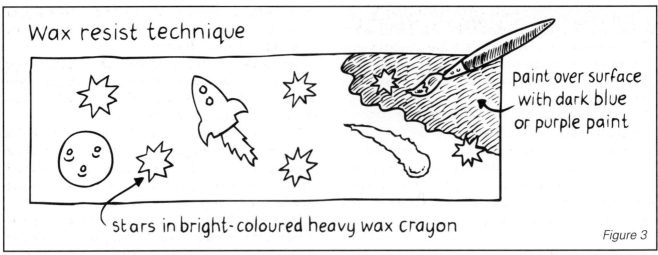

Wax resist technique

paint over surface with dark blue or purple paint

stars in bright-coloured heavy wax crayon

Figure 3

This may be a rather prescriptive way to write a poem, but it works well and gives less able children a sense of confidence and achievement.

Opportunities for IT
Some children could use a word processor to draft their poems. You could prepare a starting file to speed up the text entry process. Once the poem has been completed, the children could format it in various ways, perhaps adding clip art pictures to illustrate the different lines:

4 bright stars dancing

Display ideas
Cut out a moon shape and place it on a large sheet of paper. Spray the paper with black, purple or dark blue paint and allow to dry. Then peel off the moon shape to leave a clear white 'shadow'. Do the same thing with cut-out stars or place manufactured star shapes on the white surface – do not stick them down. Put the correct number of stars on each sheet, and write out the appropriate line of the *How many stars?* poem underneath. Again, spray dark paint over the stars and remove them when dry. (Use a paint spray with a fine nozzle and fairly thin poster paint.)

Another way to achieve this effect is to use 'wax resist' – that is, to draw the correct number of stars in bright heavy wax crayon and paint over the top with thin dark-coloured paint. (See Figure 3.)

Reference to photocopiable sheets
Photocopiable page 127 provides a writing frame. Encourage the children to write their own number poems

on this sheet, following the pattern on the flip chart and substituting new words where they can. Photocopiable page 128 provides a more prescriptive writing frame for those children who need extra support; it requires them to complete a clearly structured number poem.

THE SUN

To be introduced to the concept of image. To write image poems using a simple poetic structure.

†† *Whole class, then individual work.*

🕐 *50 minutes.*

Previous skills/knowledge needed
The children should be ready to take part in discussion and to trade ideas with others in the class. It would be useful (but is not essential) for them to be at the stage of copying a simple pattern of words from the flip chart. If necessary, the activity can be tackled on a purely oral basis.

Key background information
Image is one of the key tools of poetry writing. It is a way of making connections between one idea and another. Poetic images are usually expressed in one of two ways:
▲ Simile is a direct comparison between one thing and another, often using the word like – for example, *the moon is like a hammock*.
▲ Metaphor simply identifies one thing with another for rhetorical effect – for example, *the moon is a hammock*.

Preparation
Collect some photographs and pictures which show the sun or sunny weather. Bring in a collection of sun-related items: sunglasses, a sun-hat, sun cream and so on. Make one copy per child of photocopiable page 129.

Resources needed
Pictures and photographs of the sun, a collection of sun-related items (see 'Preparation'), a flip chart, pencils, coloured crayons or felt-tipped pens (yellow, red and orange), a daily weather chart, photocopiable page 129.

What to do
Gather the children in a semi-circle, seated where they can all see the flip chart easily. Ask the children to look outside and think about today's weather, then describe it to you. Work towards a consensus of opinion, especially if it is an 'in-between' kind of day. Ask them to decide which is the most appropriate symbol for today's weather chart.

Produce the 'sunny day items' and ask the children what kind of weather would lead them to wear these things. Look at the pictures of a sunny day – or look outside, if you are lucky! Encourage them to talk about sunshine: how hot the sun feels on their skin, how they dress to enjoy the sunshine, the perils of too much sun.

Ask the children to close their eyes and imagine the hottest day of the summer, with the sun high in the sky. Ask them to draw the shape of the sun in the air. When they open their eyes, ask them to think of something they can play with that is as round as the sun. Collect suggestions

such as *a ball, a frisbee, a hoop, a marble...* Scribe *Toys* on the flip chart and make a list of the children's suggestions. Read through the words with them.

Use the same procedure to make a list of foods that the sun is shaped like: *orange, pizza, pancake, lollipop...* Now ask the children to find some words to describe the colours of the sun: *yellow, orange, golden, red...*

You should now have three lists on the flip chart. Tell the children that all this is your 'shopping list', from which you are going to write a poem about the sun. Run through the toys they have thought of, and ask them to choose their favourite – ten to one they will say 'ball'.

Tell the children that the words they have thought of can be used to make an image or picture of the sun in their imaginations. Images are often used by poets to describe things, creating a special kind of poem: an image poem.

Scribe the first line of your image poem on the flip chart, using a simile to tells us what the sun is like – for example, *The sun is like a ball*. Now ask the children to choose a colour to go with it (remembering that they are describing the sun). The line might look like this: *The sun is like a golden ball*.

Let the children see you cross off the words as you use them – as if you were in the supermarket, putting items into your shopping trolley! Using the flip chart and scribing to their suggestions, continue until you have built a simple image poem – for example:

The sun
The sun is like a yellow ball.
It is like a golden frisbee.
The sun is like a lemon ice-cream.
It is like an orange lollipop.

If the children show that they are ready to move on to the next part of the activity, ask them to suggest flowers which are *always* round and yellow. They may suggest *marigold, primrose, dandelion, buttercup, sunflower* and so on. Use these ideas to create a final pair of lines with flower images of the sun. This time, there is no need to include the colour. Can the children explain why that is? (They have selected flowers which are always yellow.) The ending might be:

> The sun is like a buttercup.
> It is like a sunflower.

Read through the finished poem with the children. Help them to see that there is a distinct pattern: the first line of each pair starts with the words *The sun is like a...* ; the second line of each pair starts with the words *It is like...* Remind the children that they have been writing an image poem – that is, using pictures from their imaginations to make the poem work.

Give out the copies of photocopiable page 129. Ask the children to make up their own poem by filling in the gaps on the sheet. Explain that this pattern builds on the one which you have written together: it involves them finding a doing word (verb) to match each of their images. For example, if they have suggested that the sun is like a ball, they might say that it is *rolling, bouncing* or *spinning*. Then they must ask themselves *where* the ball is bouncing – and remember that they are describing the sun.

This will give the children a great deal to think about. Their first two lines might look like this:

> The sun is like a golden ball
>   rolling in the sky.

or

> The sun is like a yellow ball
>   spinning across the clouds.

They should extend the rest of the poem in a similar way:

> The sun is like a lemon ice-cream
>   melting from the sky.
> It is like a buttercup
>   dancing in the air.

Suggestion(s) for extension

Children who are independent writers may not need to use the writing frame provided on photocopiable page 129. If they do, suggest that they transform their image poems by finding some new and different sun images – extending each idea into two lines, as above. For example:

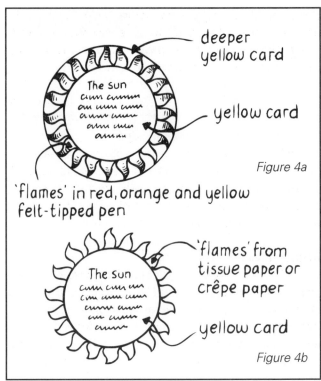

deeper
yellow card

yellow card

Figure 4a

'flames' in red, orange and yellow
felt-tipped pen

'flames' from
tissue paper or
crêpe paper

yellow card

Figure 4b

> The sun is like a shiny doorknob
>   opening the sky's door.
> It is like a goldfish
>   swimming in the air.
> The sun is like a new penny
>   dropped from the clouds.

Suggestion(s) for support

Children who lack confidence in writing independently could use the simple pattern on the flip chart. Instead of using words for their images, they could draw them (for example, a yellow ball, an orange and a dandelion). They can then read their poem aloud to a supportive adult, who can write in the missing words for the images. The children can then overwrite or underwrite the words.

Opportunities for IT

You could prepare a starting or framework file, giving the structure of the poem, in advance for the children to work on. It might look something like this:

> The sun is like...
> It is like...
> The sun is like...
> It is like...

If the word processor has a word bank facility, the words from the three lists could be stored to let the children select the word they want by clicking on it. Younger or less able children could use a concept keyboard with a prepared overlay, working with an adult to draft a poem on the

computer. More independent writers could start with the framework file, but expand it to add a second line for each simile. They could be shown how to use the 'right justify' command to format the lines of the poem:

> The sun is like a golden ball
> rolling in the sky.

The children could also use an art package to create their own pictures of the sun, related to images in their poems. These pictures could be added to the text (or the poems added to the pictures) to form part of a class display or an anthology of 'Sun' poems.

Display ideas
The children can copy out their poems onto tea-plate sized circles, mount each on a larger circle and decorate the outer rim with red, orange and yellow 'flames' (see Figure 4a). Alternatively, the flames can be cut from crêpe paper (in appropriate colours) and pasted behind the words of the poem (see Figure 4b). Arrange the children's mounted sun-image poems on a bright blue background as a wall display, above a table display of items (see 'What to do') connected with sunny weather.

Reference to photocopiable sheet
Photocopiable page 129 provides a writing frame which stimulates the children to build on the group writing task they have completed in the first half of the lesson.

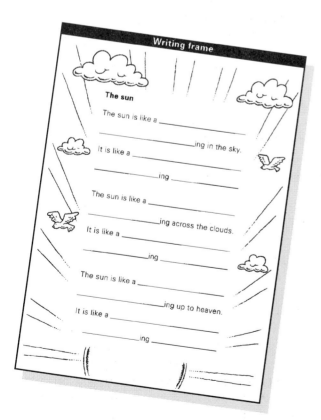

LOOKING CLOSELY

To use description and imagery to write poems based on close observation of objects.

†† Whole class, then groups.
🕘 40 minutes.

Previous skills/knowledge needed
The children should be used to discussion in a class or group situation. They should be ready to share their ideas, and have the ability to recall and talk through facts from their own experience. It would be helpful, but is not essential, for them to have some experience of using image.

Key background information
This activity encourages the children to experience some common natural objects through their senses. They should be encouraged to look closely and to touch – even to listen and smell where appropriate. They should be helped to look at everyday objects through the eyes of an artist, to investigate them as a scientist might and to describe them in the image-filled language of a poet. The initial oral activity helps to establish an outlook which can then be used in writing descriptive list poems.

Preparation
Collect a range of objects gathered from the natural environment, such as seashells, nuts, autumn leaves, stones and so on. Wrap each object in tissue paper or fine cloth, so that it can be handled unseen. Store the wrapped objects in a basket or box.

Resources needed
A basket or box of natural objects (see 'Preparation'), a flip chart, writing materials.

What to do
Seat the children in the library space and have the basket of natural resources to hand. Make sure that everyone will have a good view of your hands when you come to show and discuss the objects.

Talk with the children about times when they might receive presents: Christmas, birthdays, holidays and so on. Talk about the excitement of holding a parcel and not knowing what's inside. Ask how they go about trying to guess what it is: the shape of the parcel, its size, how heavy it is, and so on.

Suggest to the children that you are going to play a similar kind of guessing game, but not with parcels. From the basket, take out (for example) a shell wrapped in tissue paper or thin cloth. Hold it carefully and say that you are going to pass this 'mystery object' round. Tell the children that you want them to explore it with their fingers. Even if they know what it is, they mustn't say! Instead, they must

find words to describe how the object feels to them.

Let a small group of children have a go at this; then place the still-wrapped shell back in the basket. The children may suggest *hard, spiky, twirly, smooth* and so on. Scribe these words on the flip chart.

Now encourage the children to use the touch words as part of an image – for example, *hard as the pavement, hard as my head, hard as a rock... spiky as a hedgehog, spiky as a brush, spiky as a railing*. The trick is to get the children thinking about things which can be described as *hard, spiky* and so on. Work orally to begin with; then unwrap the shell and decide on the most appropriate images to go with the descriptive words suggested, scribing these images on the flip chart. You may have a list such as:

hard as a rock
spiky like a hedgehog
twirly like an ice-cream cone
smooth as glass

There will be a general shuffling about and a few comments when the shell is unwrapped: *Easy peasy! I knew what it was!* and so on. Move on to offer the shell to another small group, saying that this time they are not to use their hands to find out about the shell, but to use their eyes instead. They should look first for colour words: *creamy, pink, shiny* and so on. Help the children to develop these words into images, as they did with the touch words:

creamy as Gold Top
pink like rose petals
shiny as a star...

Explore the shell with another group to find out what else they can find to say about it, using only their eyes. They may say that it looks like *an open mouth, a deep cave, a dinosaur's back...* Scribe some of these ideas on the flip chart.

Ask another group whether the shell has a special smell. They may say that it smells *like the seaside* or *horrible* or *like fish and chips*. Add the most appropriate description to your list.

Hollow shells have a major advantage over other (non-living) objects when used in an observation session of this kind: when the children put them to their ears, they may hear *the song of the sea* or waves *whooshing* or *the sound of the wind*. Add a 'listening image' to the list.

Now let the children see you put some of their ideas together to make an image poem:

The shell
It feels spiky like a hedgehog,
as smooth as glass
and as hard as a rock.
It is creamy as Gold Top
on the outside,
pink as a rose inside.
It looks like an open mouth.
When you listen, you hear
the sound of the waves.

Let the children go through the poem with you, savouring their favourite lines or changing lines as they go along. Make a large version of the final poem for display on the wall, where everyone will be able to read and appreciate it.

Give a different wrapped object to each of the groups and ask them to describe it in a similar way, using the senses of touch, sight, smell and hearing. If there is an independent writer in each group, or an adult helper, the children's oral description can be transcribed as a 'looking closely' poem. Conclude the activity by asking each group that has a written poem to read it aloud to the others.

Suggestion(s) for extension

Give pairs of independent writers an everyday object from the kitchen, garden or classroom, such as a flowerpot, a can-opener or a pencil sharpener. Encourage them to imagine that they have never seen such a thing before, and to describe it using their senses. They could write down appropriate touch images, colour images, shape images and so on, then use them to create a *What is it?* poem:

It feels smooth as a mirror,
pointed like a mountain,
with ridges like a cliff.
It is shiny as a star,
silvery like a jewel.
It looks like a wigwam
standing in a pond.
It smells of marmalade.
It belongs in the kitchen.
What is it?
(Answer: a lemon squeezer.)

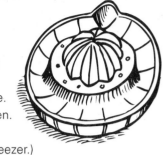

Suggestion(s) for support

Children who are not yet confident of their independent writing skills could work with an adult helper. For example, taking a wrapped-up stone, the helper could ask *What does this feel like?* If the question elicits only 'hard', the helper could try giving alternatives – for example, *Is it heavy or light?* or *Is it rough or smooth?* Next, he or she should ask about the object's shape. At this stage, he or she could scribe the responses *hard, heavy, smooth, round.*

Now the helper should ask a child to unwrap the stone, and invite suggestions about its colour – *grey with a white stripe, the colour of my Nan's hair, like a spider's web.* The question *What does it look like?* may be a difficult question for children who need support, because to them it may simply look 'like a stone'. They should be encouraged to build on this: *stones on the shore, a doorstop, the moon.*

Finally, the helper should scribe a simple poem which the children can read – for example:

The stone

It is hard and heavy.
It is round and smooth.
It is the colour of
a spider's web.
It looks like a rock
from outer space.

Opportunities for IT

An adult helper could use a word processor to scribe the children's ideas about their mystery object. The resulting ideas can be put together to make up a 'mystery poem' – fun even when it doesn't make sense! The children could experiment with different arrangements of lines to see which they like the most and which sounds the most logical.

Display ideas

The children should be encouraged to follow up their observational writing with an observational drawing session. They should use a pencil to draw shells, stones, pieces of driftwood and so on from the originals, as accurately as they can. Their pencil drawings can be mounted on black card for display. The children could use coloured pencils or crayons to illustrate the poems about garden, classroom and kitchen utensils.

AT THE SEASIDE

To develop their ability to recognize and use descriptive language through writing a list poem with a repetitive pattern.

†† *Whole class, then individual work.*

🕐 *50 minutes.*

Previous skills/knowledge needed

The children should be used to sharing their ideas with others in the class. They should know something about what can be found at the seaside, and be able to explore the content of a picture.

Key background information

This activity teaches something about adjectives, nouns and verbs although is unnecessary to name the parts of speech at this stage. Encourage the children to explore language and don't accept the first descriptive word offered. Much of the language teaching is in the oral exchange of ideas. This pattern can be used with success again and again for a range of different themes. This activity works particularly well after a class visit to the seaside; but photocopiable page 130 provides a good substitute.

Preparation

Make an enlarged (A3) copy or OHT of photocopiable page 130. With the children's help, make a collection of 'seaside' objects: a bucket and spade, a fishing net, a sun-hat, shells, a picnic basket and so on.

Resources needed

Photocopiable page 130, a collection of 'seaside' objects, a flip chart and coloured marker pens (or chalkboard and coloured chalk), blank A4 paper, writing materials.

What to do

Gather the children together in the library corner. Show them the bucket and spade, and ask where they would be likely to use these. Discuss visits to the seaside, taking time to listen to an exchange of holiday memories. Give as many children as possible the opportunity to participate.

Look at the other things in the 'seaside' collection, asking the children to say (for example) where they might find shells, when it would be sensible to wear a sun-hat, what they might catch in the net (suggesting that they return any living creatures to the sea), what they would need to build a sandcastle, and so on.

Now show the children the seaside picture (on photocopiable page 130), asking the children to explore it with their eyes, but not to comment or ask questions. Tell them that they have two minutes to find as many things that belong to the seaside as they can. When the time is up, ask the children to tell you some of the things they have seen in the picture. From their answers, scribe a list of six fairly different objects (nouns) in the middle of the flip chart using a coloured marker pen (for example, red).

When you have finished, read through the list with the children. It might look something like this:

sun
fish
boats
children
gulls
waves

Tell the children whose suggestions you have not used to keep their ideas inside their heads for later on.

Now look for words to describe what the things look like – for example, to describe the sun, a child might suggest *yellow*. What other words describe the sun? *Bright, round, golden, hot, shiny...* Choose a word from the list and scribe (for example) *golden sun* using a different-coloured marker. Go down the list, choosing an adjective for each noun. Don't take the first word offered: 'trade words' with the children so that you are consciously extending their knowledge and understanding of language.

Now your list might look something like this:

golden sun
silver fish
painted boats
happy children
noisy gulls
lacy waves

Again, remind the children to keep their unused words and ideas locked safely in their heads until they are needed later on.

Now ask the children for words which say what these things are doing (verbs). For example, they might suggest that the *golden sun* is *shining, burning, glowing, shimmering, floating, blazing, glittering* and so on. Let the children see how much you enjoy listening to and saying all the different words, and how exciting it is to find so many. Make this part of the activity one of discovery and shared enjoyment.

Now, using a different-coloured marker, scribe a third version of the word list – for example:

golden sun shimmering
silver fish jumping
painted boats rocking
happy children laughing
noisy gulls screaming
lacy waves splashing

If they haven't already noticed, point out to the children that each line ends with a word that ends in *-ing*.

Read through the list with the children, and tell them that the words nearly make a poem. It still needs to be 'topped and tailed'. Find a title with which the children are happy (such as *On the beach* or *Portrait of the seashore*) and scribe it at the top. Then add an opening question, such as *Can you see...?* or *What's on the beach?* or *Is it a day for...?* Add a question mark to each line, and comment on why we use these marks. Finally, add a couplet to finish off the poem, such as *Here we are down by the sea. / I wish that you could be with me!* or *We like to play out in the sun. / Watch us having lots of fun!*

The completed poem should have a different colour for each part of speech (adjectives, nouns and verbs). It might look something like this:

At the seaside

Can you see
the golden sun shining?
silver fish jumping?
painted boats rocking?
happy children laughing?
noisy gulls screaming?
lacy waves splashing?
We like to play out in the sun.
Watch us having lots of fun!

Give out blank sheets of A4 paper. Ask the children to fold their sheet down the middle, then draw vertical lines in pencil to divide the whole page into three columns (see Figure 5). When they are ready, ask the children to choose four 'red words' (nouns) and write them in a list down the middle of the page, across the fold. They can choose any 'red words' from the flip chart, or write down something else which they can see in the picture – perhaps something they have kept inside their heads from earlier on. Go over any new nouns with them (for example, *shells, umbrellas, buckets, balloons* or *kites*).

Now ask the children to move to the left-hand column and write in some 'green words' (adjectives) – so they could write *silver balloons, happy waves, painted buckets* and so on. Then they should choose 'blue words' (verbs) from the *-ing* list, making three-word lines. Finally, they should top and tail their poems – either with their own ideas or with phrases from the flip chart.

Have a read-around of the finished poems, letting the children see how much you appreciate their use of original or unusual language – for example, comment on how *green waves dancing* or *curly shells shining* creates a picture in the listener's mind.

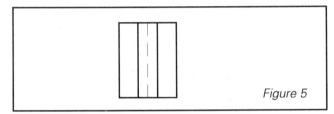

Figure 5

Suggestion(s) for extension

Children who are confident writers could try extending their lines to suggest places – for example:

> happy children playing
> on the sand
> blue boats bouncing
> on the waves
> silver fish swimming
> in the sea
> white gulls gliding
> in the sky

Suggestion(s) for support

Children who need help with their writing could concentrate on writing a simple noun and adjective list – for example:

> Can you see
> hot sun?
> happy children?
> noisy gulls?
> red boats?
> That's what I see
> at the seaside.

Assessment opportunities

Look for children who know, understand and can use unusual words, especially verbs. Note those who can reject an inappropriate word combination (such as *shells dancing* or *crabs singing*) and can find suitable alternatives... that is, unless they knowingly make their poem into a magical and mysterious piece!

Opportunities for IT

Some children could write their poems on a word processor. They will need to be able to see the class list of words. If the word processing software uses frames or tables, you could set up a framework file with columns (like the folded paper used in the main activity). Thus a child might key in:

Golden	sun	shining
Silver	fish	jumping

The framework boundary lines can be turned off in the final poem.

Display ideas

The children can make a seaside scene on a long roll of blue frieze paper. For the background, they can show the sand area using dabs of yellow, gold and brown paint (in a pointillist style) and overlap 'waves' of silver, blue and green translucent paper or foil. A round yellow sun can be added high in the sky; children, boats and gulls can be painted, cut out and stuck on the seaside background. The children's poems can be placed around the frieze, and a display of buckets, spades, shells, stones, nets and so on can be arranged on a table beneath it.

Reference to photocopiable sheet

The picture on photocopiable page 130 is a 'starter' for creative writing. It should be used to elicit words for a list poem; the children can then select items from the list on the flip chart to construct their own poems.

At the seaside

OPPOSITES

To write patterned poems based on the idea of contrast, using a range of descriptive vocabulary.
†† *Whole class, then individual work.*
🕐 *45 minutes.*

Previous skills/knowledge needed

The children should be used to sharing their ideas with others in the class. They should know something about opposites, and have the appropriate vocabulary to explore the idea of contrast in relation to their everyday lives.

Key background information

The idea of contrast is a useful teaching tool. Exploring a theme through its opposite, balancing one with the other, can heighten the effect of both. This activity encourages an exploration of vocabulary; the children should be helped to look for words and phrases which will deepen and enhance vivid description.

Preparation

Gather some photographs and pictures which illustrate contrasts: night and day, winter and summer, large and small (for example, large and small dogs), and so on. Collect a few items which have a contrasting texture (for example, rough and smooth). Make one copy per child of photocopiable page 131.

Resources needed

Contrasting pictures and photographs (see 'Preparation'), objects with contrasting textures, photocopiable page 131, a flip chart, writing materials.

What to do

Gather the children in the story or library corner, where everyone can sit comfortably. Tell them that you have some pictures for them to look at: they should explore the pictures with their eyes and search for details, but not comment aloud until later on.

Hold up a 'night' picture in one hand and a 'day' one in the other. Ask the children what they can see in the pictures – for example, *I can see the moon and the stars in one picture, but it's sunny in the other one. One picture is dark, one is light. It's daytime in one picture, night in the other.* Show two contrasting winter and summer pictures. Talk with the children about contrasts, and elicit the word 'opposite'.

Explore more opposite ideas by asking: *What is the opposite of high? ...of fast? ...of young?* and so on. Encourage the children to offer their own sets of opposites, such as *large and small, short and tall, big and little* (is that the same as *large and small*?), *hard and soft, black and white...* Spend a few minutes on this oral exercise.

Now let the children examine the objects, using their fingers to explore 'opposite' textures and finding appropriate 'touch words': *rough, bumpy, knobbly* and *smooth, slippery, silky...* Encourage them to talk about things which feel rough or smooth – for example, *rough like my Grandad's cheeks...* or *prickly...* or *scratchy; smooth as a pebble...* or *shiny...* or *polished...* The children might decide that the opposite of *prickly* is *polished*, the opposite of *scratchy* is *shiny*, and so on. Make this a creative exploration of language.

Return to the day and night pictures. Ask the children to look for pairs of words which describe opposites in the

two pictures, such as *dark/light, moonlight/sunlight, sleeping/awake...* Scribe some of the children's suggestions on the flip chart.

Ask the children about the sounds they might hear at night – *cats meowing, owls hooting, babies crying, parents snoring, policemen walking...* And in the day: *traffic roaring, people talking, children playing, dogs barking, dustbin lorries turning, concrete mixers whirring, telephones ringing...* Scribe some of their ideas on the flip chart.

Tell the children that you have chosen a line with which to begin a poem – for example, *In the day*. Ask the children how they could build up the poem using some of the ideas on the flip chart – for example:

In the day
people talk,
children play,
telephones ring,
traffic speeds...
The street is busy.

With the children's help, build up a contrasting verse about night. Write it beside the first verse on the flip chart. You may wish to change some of the lines as you go along. The result could be:

In the night
babies cry,
birds are silent,
children sleep,
cats walk...
The street is quiet.

Show the children how you have matched the second verse to the first: similar opening lines, four short lines with examples of things that happen, then similar endings.

Work through another version of the same poem – for example:

In the day,	In the night,
the sun shines,	the moon gleams,
birds sing,	owls hoot,
squirrels jump,	bats fly,
trees are bright...	trees are dark...
The forest is awake.	The forest sleeps.

Next, show the children contrasting pictures of summer and winter. As before, compile lists of opposites or contrasts relating to the weather, clothes, colours, sounds, the trees and so on. Explain that you are going to make up another 'opposites' poem, using the same pattern as before. Ask them to help you find a suitable opening line for each verse – for example, *In the summer* and *In the winter* or *Summer is* and *Winter is*. The poem might look like this:

On summer days	On winter days
the sun shines,	the snow falls,
trees are green,	trees are bare,
birds sing out loud	birds hide away
and I wear my shorts	and I wear my scarf
and sun-hat.	and bobble hat.
Summer days are warm.	Winter days are cold.

Give out copies of photocopiable page 131. Ask the children to make up their own 'day and night' poems, using the sheet as a writing frame. Let them have another long look at the two pictures. Explain that they should fill in the four lines in each verse, using some of the ideas from the flip chart – or, even better, some new ideas of their own. They should finish the last lines of the two verses with words that mean the opposite to each other – for example:

▲ *The street is busy* and *The street is lonely.*
▲ *The street is noisy* and *The street is silent.*
▲ *The street is crowded* and *The street is empty.*

Conclude the activity by asking some of the children to read their 'day and night' poems aloud. Encourage them to express the verses differently – perhaps by sounding upbeat and excited in the 'daytime' verse and using a soft, sleepy voice for the 'night' verse.

Suggestion(s) for extension

Children who are independent writers could explore other contrasting ideas to create poems – *springtime and autumn, rough and smooth* (using some of the texture vocabulary from earlier in the activity), *fast and slow, old and young,* and so on. Remind them to make up lists of contrasting ideas and 'opposite' words before they begin. The poem should then follow the pattern demonstrated on the flip chart – for example:

POETRY

Fast and slow

Through the air	Along the lanes
aeroplanes zoom,	ponies plod,
jets speed,	tractors rumble,
satellites spin	dogs amble
and rockets whizz	and people stroll
leaving sparks.	picking flowers.

The trick with this particular poem is to find words which give the impression of speed (*zoom, speed, spin, whizz*) and contrast these with slow-sounding words (*plod, rumble, amble, stroll*).

Suggestion(s) for support

Children who need a helping hand with independent writing could work with a supportive adult. He or she should work through a 'night and day' shared poem, emphasizing the steps:

1. Scribe the possibilities for the children, asking questions such as: *What things or people do you see in the street during the day?...at night? What do they do?*
2. Let the children choose phrases from these lists and copy them onto photocopiable page 131.
3. Help them to find contrasting end-words for the two verses.
4. Encourage them to read their poems aloud, as the others have done. Give assistance if necessary.

Assessment opportunities

Look for those children who have an extensive vocabulary and can recognize synonyms. Note which children can construct their own 'opposites' poems, following the structure given.

Opportunities for IT

Some children could use a word processor to write their poems. To help them place the two poems side by side, show them how to use the Tab key to shift the writing along the page. You may need to set the tabs before the children start. An example might be:

In the day	In the night
the sun shines	the moon gleams

Explain to the children why it is better to use the Tab key rather than the SPACE bar:

▲ It always moves automatically to the correct place, so the starting words are correctly lined up under each other.
▲ If you change your mind, you can alter the tab positions using the ruler and all of the column will change.
▲ It takes account of the fact that letters vary in width, whereas it is often impossible to make the letters line up correctly using the SPACE bar.

An alternative approach, when the word processor has a table facility (or when the children are using frames), is to set up two columns:

On summer days	On winter days
The sun shines	The snow falls
Trees are green	Trees are bare

The frame borders can be turned off when the poem has been written.

Display ideas

The children can cut their completed photocopiable sheets in half or write out their 'day and night' poems in best, then paste the daytime verse onto yellow card and the night verse onto black card. They can work together to paint a huge orange sun on a blue backing sheet, and a white or silver moon on a purple backing sheet; then each poem can be pasted onto the appropriate backing sheet.

Performance ideas

The children can read their contrasting poems aloud to an audience, varying their delivery to heighten the contrasts.

Reference to photocopiable sheet

Photocopiable page 131 should be used as a writing frame for a poem. The children should fill in the blank lines with contrasting images taken from the flip chart or their own imaginations. The words added to end the two verses should be opposites (as in *noisy* and *silent*).

POEMS IN COLOUR

To write a group poem based on a listing technique. To compare this with a published poem on the same theme, looking at structure, language and rhyme.

†† *Whole class, then individual work.*

⏰ *45 minutes.*

Previous skills/knowledge needed
The children should be used to sharing ideas and volunteering information. They should be familiar with the names of colours. They should know about some common fruits and wildflowers, and be able to identify them from pictures or samples.

Key background information
This activity is based on listing, and offers a way into a simple poetry structure which can be used for almost any topic at Key Stage 1.

Preparation
Make a simple collection of things in one colour – red is a likely favourite among young children. Gather, for example, a lipstick, a tomato, strawberries and/or some appropriate pictures (a post-box, poppies, the setting sun and so on). Make an enlarged (A3) copy or OHT of photocopiable page 132, and make one A4 copy per child. Find books which include more poems about colour (for example, *The First Lick of the Lolly* edited by Moira Andrew, Macmillan 1986).

Resources needed
A 'colour' collection (see 'Preparation'), photocopiable page 132, a classroom colour chart, a flip chart, writing materials, poetry collections and anthologies.

What to do
Seat the children comfortably in the library area and make sure that everyone has a clear view of the flip chart. Introduce the activity by talking about the objects you have gathered together – but do not specifically mention colour. Examine each item in turn and ask the children whether they can find something to say about it. If nobody has said anything about colour, ask the children whether they can see something that is the same about all the things in the collection. *They are all red – of course!*

Ask the children whether they can think of other things that are always red – raspberries, stop lights, flames, holly berries and so on. List these things on the flip chart, and add the names of some of the red items in the collection.

Use the list to demonstrate how to build up a colour poem. Tell the children that the poem will answer the question, *What is red?* The list might be as follows: *tomatoes, holly berries, flames, foxgloves, post-boxes, cherries, ladybirds, poppies, lipstick...* quite a mixture! Scribe *What is red?* and ask the children to choose an item from the list: *Holly berries are red* or *The post-box is red.*

Write *and* before scribing another item from the list. This time, the children should say something more about it – for example, *Poppies have bright red petals. They grow in our garden.* With the children's help, select parts of this description to fit into two short lines in the verse, scribing on the flip chart as each suggestion is made. For example:

Holly berries are red	The post-box is red
and bright poppies	and the light that tells
growing in the garden.	the cars to stop.

Build up a poem on the flip chart in this way, scribing four verses that follow a three-line pattern – for example:

What is red?
Holly berries are red
and bright poppies
growing in the garden.
    The post-box is red
    and the light that tells
    the cars to stop.
        Cherries are red
        and juicy strawberries
        covered with cream.
            Flames are red
            and a ladybird's back
            with black spots on.

Read out the poem 'Colours' from the enlarged version of photocopiable page 132. When you have finished, look at the pattern the poem makes on the page. Explain to the children what a **verse** is, and count the number of verses. Compare the appearance of the poem on the flip chart with that of 'Colours'. There are four verses in each; but 'Colours' has four lines in each verse, whereas 'What is red?' has only three.

Explore other differences between the two poems. 'Colours' asks a question in the first line of each verse, and looks at three different colours (and a rainbow); 'What is red?' uses the title to ask one question only, and concentrates on a single colour. Ask the children which poem rhymes. Look for the rhyming words: *tree/see* and *hot/not* in 'Colours'.

Give out copies of photocopiable page 132. Let the children use this and the structure you have demonstrated to make up their own versions of *What is red?* Allow them to read their own poems to the rest of the class if they wish.

Finally, organize a class reading of 'Colours' with everyone asking the questions and a different group giving each reply. Follow the same procedure with the poem on the flip chart. Ask the children to tell you which poem they like more and why.

Suggestion(s) for extension

Ask children who are independent writers to gather a list of things which are always yellow, always blue or always green. Go over the way in which the poem 'What is red?' is structured, and ask the children to write a poem about another colour in the same way. Suggest a maximum of two verses for each colour – for example:

What is yellow?
The sun is yellow
and buttercups
   dancing in the field.

  Lemons are yellow
  and dandelions
    growing in the grass.

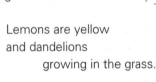

Suggestion(s) for support

Help those children who need support to work on a group poem instead of individual poems. Initially, suggest a list of possible green objects such as *grass, leaves, Christmas trees, the light that says 'Go'*... Scribe two-line verses from their dictation, putting the phrase *and so is* or *and so are* at the beginning of each second line – for example:

What is green?
Leaves are green
and so is a Christmas tree.
  Grass is green
  and so is the 'Go' light.

Let these children read their poem aloud to the others, perhaps taking one line each.

Opportunities for IT

Some children could use a word processor to write their poems. In order to set out each verse indented from the previous one, they should use the Tab command to line up their writing rather than the Space bar (see page 64).

Display ideas

A display in several colours could include fruits and flowers, pictures and posters, (unopened) pots of paint and so on, with the items in each colour gathered beneath poems copied out in red, blue, yellow or green felt-tipped pen. Title the whole display 'Colour', and scribe *What is red? ...blue? ...yellow?* or *...green?* above each panel. An overarching rainbow could give the display an effective frame.

Performance ideas

Give the children minimal costumes in different colours – for example, hats made of crêpe paper in each of the colours in the children's poems. A performing group should ask the questions (for example, *What is red?*), and the correctly dressed child should answer individually with lines from the appropriate poems.

Reference to photocopiable sheet

The poem on photocopiable page 132 can be enlarged to A3 size, or copied onto an OHT, for display during the lesson. Individual copies will be useful for closer study of the poem's structure, and for reading aloud.

Colour poem

Colours

What is green?
The grass is green,
and leaves upon
a tree.

What is blue?
The sky is blue,
as anyone
can see.

What is red?
A fire is red
when it is burning
hot;

And what has ALL
the colours in?
A RAINBOW,
has it not?

by Jean Kenward

Using a Pattern

Using a repetitive poetry pattern allows young children to try out different strategies and techniques within a familiar framework – though they will need to be reminded of the 'rules' before they start. This helps to give them confidence, and makes them less inhibited about putting words on paper.

Some of the patterns in these activities rely on a simple one-word substitution. For example, in 'Days of the week' (page 71), the children already know the days of the week (or can follow a chart), so their ideas can be fitted into the pattern to produce an original poem. This looks easy, and encourages participation from even the most reluctant writer.

A more complex pattern might depend on a standard phrase followed by an image. If the children are aware that the first line of each verse begins with *The sun is like...*, everyone knows where to begin. They can copy these words and concentrate on the image that follows. This method works well if the children have contributed to a list of similes which the teacher has scribed on the flip chart. The children will have the satisfaction of creating an original image poem – no two will be the same!

Encourage the children to experiment with various poetic patterns and structures. For example, find poems which contain number sequences or follow the seasons, and suggest substitutions which the children might try. Far from inhibiting creativity, this method often releases interesting language and new ideas, especially among those who need support with poetry writing. Let the children share and exchange ideas, stand patterns on their heads and turn them inside-out. The results will surprise and excite you.

POETRY

WHO LIVES HERE?

To use a simple, repetitive poem as a model for composing patterned poems by introducing new words.

†† *Whole class and groups.*

🕐 *40 minutes.*

Previous skills/knowledge needed

The children should have some knowledge of animal homes. This can be reinforced by the use of appropriate pictures and posters. They should be used to listening to and sharing poems, and should be ready to join in with their own ideas and suggestions.

Key background information

This activity provides a simple repetitive pattern which gives the children confidence in writing a poem and encourages their participation. It can be successful on a purely oral basis, but the structure is simple enough for newly independent writers to add new lines of their own invention. All the children should be able to join in the choral element of the poem, and the repeated phrases make it a relatively 'easy read'.

Preparation

Make an enlarged (A3) copy or OHT of photocopiable page 133. Make some copies of photocopiable page 134 (see 'Suggestion(s) for support). Find some pictures or posters of familiar animal homes, such as a bird's nest, a spider's web, a beehive, a pond and so on.

Resources needed

Photocopiable pages 133 and 134, pictures or posters of familiar animal homes, a flip chart; writing materials (see 'Suggestion(s) for extension'); drawing materials (see 'Suggestion(s) for support').

What to do

Gather the children in the library or a similar carpeted area. Make sure they are all comfortably seated and ready to listen, and that they are all in a position to see the pictures and posters.

Talk about the homes that people live in: houses, flats, bungalows, trailers, caravans and so on. Elicit the children's awareness that their homes keep out the elements and provide warmth and safety. Home is a place to eat, sleep and play; and each home has its own identity. Discuss with the children the similarities and differences between the places where they live. For example, they all have doors and windows; but they have different numbers on their doors, probably the colour of the paint (outside or inside) is different, and no two gardens look the same!

Show the children pictures of various animals' homes. Establish that a spider lives in a web, a bird in a nest and so on. Ask whether the children know about other animal homes, including ones built by people such as a pigsty, rabbit hutch, dog kennel or cowshed.

Tell the children that you are going to read them a poem called 'Who lives here?' Tell them that this is a poem full of questions – but you are sure they will know all the answers! Read out the first verse; then say that you will repeat the first part of the verse and the children should say the closing

words: *'I do,' said the spider / 'This is my home!'*

Use the same technique for the next three verses, letting the children choose a different creature if appropriate. For example, *Who lives in the pond...?* could be a tadpole, a frog or a water boatman, rather than a *fish* as in the original poem. When you reach the final verse, read it through so that the children know how it goes, then let them join in.

Let the children see the enlarged version of the poem and suggest that they read it in groups, taking a verse each – or with one group asking the questions and another providing the answers.

Encourage the children to suggest new ideas for homes – for example: *Who lives in the burrow? Who lives in the grass? Who lives in the sea? Who lives in the hive?* When they have answered these questions, go on to help them extend each idea into a second line which says where they will find the home – for example, *Who lives in the burrow / underneath the hill?* or *Who lives in the burrow / deep down in the earth?*

Scribe one of the children's ideas on the flip chart in full and read it together, so that you have a new verse such as this:

> Who lives in the burrow
> hidden on the common?
> 'I do,' said the rabbit,
> 'This is my home!'

From the children's suggestions, scribe several more new verses. Encourage the more inventive or unusual ideas, such as:

> Who lives in the sett,
> buried deep in the woods?
> 'I do,' said the badger,
> 'This is my home!'

When you have created four new verses, divide the children into four groups. Ask each group to read out two verses: one from the original poem and one new one. All the groups should finish by reading out the last verse (about their own home) together, pointing to themselves as they reach the final line.

Suggestion(s) for extension

The more confident children could create farmyard versions of 'Who lives here?', incorporating animal homes created by people:

> Who lives in the stable
> by the farmer's yard?
> 'I do,' said the horse,
> 'This is my home!'

Children who are independent writers could write out their own farmyard verse, following the pattern on the flip chart. An adult should scribe from the children's dictation if they are not at this stage.

Suggestion(s) for support

Children who need support could work with photocopiable page 134. On the picture of the web, they should draw a spider; in the nest, they should draw a bird and so on. They should copy the line *This is my home!* on the blank line underneath each of their drawings.

Assessment opportunities

Note those children who can use a simple pattern as the basis for their own independent writing. Look for those who can extend their lines by suggesting where the homes are to be found.

Opportunities for IT

The groups of children who have made up new verses for the poem could read their verses into a cassette recorder. They could also word-process their text and use it as a reading text with the cassette recorder. The text and cassette can be added to the listening corner.

Alternatively, the children could use a multimedia authoring package to create a simple talking book. They could record their verses using a microphone attached to the computer. Each verse could be written and formatted on a page in the presentation, with a sound file linked to it. As the reader 'turns over' the pages, the voices of the children reciting the verses they have created will be heard. Replay arrows could be added, so that children can read and listen to the book again. The page could be illustrated with simple pictures taken from clip art collections, drawn using an art package, photographed with a digital camera or scanned from the children's own line drawings.

Display ideas

Give each child a sheet of art or sugar paper folded into a four-page double zigzag book, with a flap cut into each page. (See Figure 1.) They can choose four animal homes and draw one on the outside of each flap; then inside, they can draw a picture of the appropriate creature (for example, a hive on the outside and a bee on the inside). They can copy the words *This is my home!* as a speech bubble coming from the mouth of each creature. When the flap is lifted, the occupant appears inside! On the title page, the children can write *Who lives here?* and, most importantly, the name of the book's author; they can add drawings of various animals as appropriate.

Performance ideas

The groups (see 'What to do') can perform the verses which they have made up for themselves, and all the children can join in the chorus.

Reference to photocopiable sheets

Photocopiable page 133 should be copied onto an A3 sheet or OHT for display during the lesson. Children who need support with reading and writing can use photocopiable page 134, drawing appropriate animals and copying the line *This is my home!* under each animal picture.

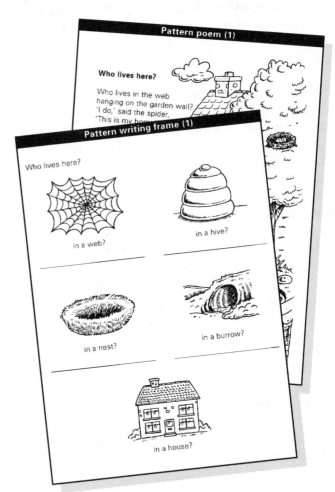

Figure 1

DAYS OF THE WEEK

To construct a simple sequential poem through shared composition, based on a published poem. To learn and recite a simple sequential poem.

†† *Whole class, then individual work.*

⏱ *30 minutes.*

Previous skills/knowledge needed

It would be helpful, but is not essential, for the children to know the sequence of the days of the week. They should be able to listen to poems and stories being read aloud, and be prepared to contribute their ideas to a class discussion.

Key background information

This activity is an early introduction to sequencing in poetry. It gives the children confidence in planning their writing and working to an established structure.

Preparation

Make an enlarged (A3) copy or OHT of photocopiable page 135. Make one copy per child of photocopiable page 136. Find some books of nursery rhymes, such as *Lavender's Blue* compiled by Kathleen Lines (OUP, 1989).

Resources needed

A wall chart showing the days of the week, a board or flip chart, pencils, coloured pencils or crayons, a selection of nursery rhyme books, photocopiable pages 135 and 136.

What to do

Gather the children in the story corner and make sure that they are comfortable. By asking questions, establish with the children what day of the week it is. Using the 'Days of the week' wall chart, consolidate the concept of yesterday, today and tomorrow. Go on to ask, for example, *If today was Thursday, what day would yesterday/tomorrow be?*

Follow this procedure with all the days of the week, encouraging the children to sight-read the names of the days.

Introduce the nursery rhyme or song *How many days?* Ask the children to clap out the rhythm and repeat the rhyme with you:

How many days has my baby to play?
Saturday, Sunday, Monday,
Tuesday, Wednesday, Thursday, Friday,
Saturday, Sunday, Monday.

Go on to substitute new verses – for example: *How many days has my granny to knit? How many days has my budgie to sing? How many days has my kitten to pounce?* and so on.

This rhyme helps to establish in the children's minds the fact that each week has seven days, and that these days come in a sequence and start again. Read aloud some other nursery rhymes based on the days of the week, such as *They that wash on Monday* and *Solomon Grundy, born on Monday.*

Ask the children to think about what makes each day of the week different. The weekend days are easy; mid-week days are much harder to distinguish. Use the flip chart to scribe some of the children's ideas for each day: **Monday**, *back to school, Granny's washing day, the day I go to music lessons;* **Tuesday**, *singing in the hall, PE, the day we visit Uncle Albert...* and so on.

Now read John Cotton's poem 'The Week' (see photocopiable page 135) aloud. Then ask the children to join in, following the words on the enlarged version. Ask them how each line begins. Help them to see that the poem has a pattern: *As ... as Monday / As ... as Tuesday*, and so on.

Encourage the children to memorize and recite the poem. With its sequence of days and every line starting with *As,* they should find it a fairly easy task. Tell them that

POETRY

this is a practice run-through, and that you will work on it together again later.

The children will have commented (earlier) that they go back to school on Mondays after the weekend. Encourage them to suggest words to describe what kind of day a Monday usually is – for example, *busy, boring, hard-working...* Suggest that they use one of these words to make the beginning of a new poem following the original pattern – for example, *As busy as Monday* or *As boring as Monday*.

With the children's help, search for words to describe the rest of the week. Scribe at least three ideas under each day's heading on the flip chart. When you have listed words for each day in the week, give out copies of photocopiable page 136; ask the children to fill in the missing words, creating their own poem. It might look like this:

As busy as Monday
As terrific as Tuesday
As lucky as Wednesday
As funny as Thursday
As tiring as Friday
As fantastic as Saturday
As quiet as Sunday

If you have scribed a number of possibilities for each day in the week, no two of the children's poems should turn out quite the same.

Take time to read some of the children's work aloud, commenting in particular on any unusual words which they have used. This should be a brief session of sharing and congratulations. Conclude the lesson by returning to the original poem and encouraging all the children to memorize and recite it.

Suggestion(s) for extension

Children who are independent writers could make up a new poem by looking for the 'dark' side of each day until they get to the weekend – for example:

Monday is a boring day
Tuesday is a terrible day
Wednesday is a worse day
Thursday is an awful day
Friday is a frightful day
    But ...
Saturday is a sporty day
And Sunday is a super day,
    The best day of all!

If they like, these children could write out their finished poems as an eight-page zigzag book, using the first page for the title.

Suggestion(s) for support

Children who need support with writing can use the classroom 'Days of the week' chart to help with the words. Encourage them to match the names of the days on the chart to those in the poem, in order to build up confidence, before they work on the writing task. Give help and support as they continue.

Assessment opportunities

Note which children are familiar with the sequence of days in the week. Look for those who can find interesting and unusual describing words.

Opportunities for IT

The children could use a word processor to originate their own poems. If you provide a template file with the structure of the poem already created, the children can retrieve this and use it as a basis for their writing. This will help them to concentrate on the descriptive aspect, and will encourage them to try different words. If the word processor has a word bank facility, the class list of words can be added to it to make the writing task easier. The children could work in pairs, with each child making a slightly different version of the poem from a common starting point. The framework file might look like this:

As   as Monday
As   as Tuesday

The children could experiment with different fonts and colours to give their final poems more impact.

Display ideas

Using large sheets of sugar paper or card, make a different-coloured backing sheet for each day of the week. The children can paint and cut out figures doing different activities for each day, then glue them collage-style onto the backing sheets. They can make a large label for each day, perhaps using the word processor. An enlarged (A3) copy of John Cotton's poem can be placed at one end of the display, and some of the children's poems at the other end.

Performance ideas

While an adult or a confident child reads out rhymes which refer to the days of the week, the children can role-play appropriate actions or postures (for example, *Monday's child is fair of face*). If they have learned John Cotton's poem, they can include this as part of the performance.

Reference to photocopiable sheets

Photocopiable page 135 should be copied onto an A3 sheet or OHT for display during the lesson. Photocopiable page 136 is a writing frame based on the poem on page 135; the children should fill in the gaps with words they have chosen.

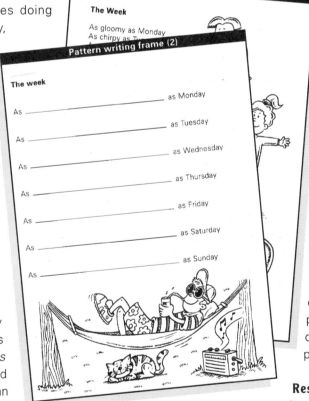

IN ONE SECOND

To use a repetitive poetry pattern, substituting their own ideas for parts of the original poem. To read their own poems aloud.

✝✝ *Whole class, groups, then individual work.*

🕐 *40 minutes.*

Previous skills/knowledge needed

The children should understand how time is measured in seconds, minutes and hours. They should know that clocks and watches are used to tell the time. They should be used to listening and taking part in class discussions.

Key background information

This activity is structured to allow the children to create their own pieces of writing through substitution. The simple list poem used as a pattern works well if read as a 'round' by groups of children. In this activity, the children will need to estimate time passing – for example, the time it takes to perform a simple action and how many things they can do in a minute. You may find that the children have great difficulty in making anything like an accurate estimate of how time passes.

Preparation

Plan some easily-organized activities which will give the children an idea of one second, such as untying a shoe lace, closing a book, opening a bottle of pop, biting a biscuit or switching a light on/off. Collect a variety of instruments for measuring seconds – clocks, watches, an egg-timer, a stop-watch and so on – and a variety of percussion instruments. Make an enlarged (A3) copy or OHT of photocopiable page 137. Make one copy per child of photocopiable page 138.

Resources needed

Clocks, watches, an egg-timer, a stop-watch and other instruments for measuring time (see 'Preparation'), some percussion instruments, a flip chart, photocopiable pages 137 and 138.

What to do

Gather the children together in the story corner. Ask them:
▲ *What things do we use to tell the time?*

▲ *Can anyone say what time it is now?*

If a child is wearing a watch, let him or her tell the others what time it is. Look at the classroom clock, and then at your own watch. Is the time the same?

Show the children the various clocks and watches which you have assembled. Discuss when these are used, who uses them and how they are different. Show the children how clocks and watches measure hours, minutes and seconds, and how you can sometimes see the seconds passing by. Talk about other places where the time is shown: on the cooker, the video, the computer and so on. *When is it important to know the correct time? –* when you have to catch a train, when you are baking a cake, when it's time for school, and so on.

Talk about different times of the day: getting up, breakfast, school time, break, lunchtime, bedtime and so on. Ask the children whether they know how long it is between now and break: *an hour, ten minutes, five minutes, one minute, one second?* Take the best guess – for example, *about an hour* – and encourage the children to think of other things that take 'about an hour': to go from school to town, to get to Grandma's house, to walk across the park and back, and so on.

AAA-CHOO!!

Show the children the stop-watch. Talk about how important it is for timing athletes or for timing boiled eggs, cakes and so on. Now tell them that you are going to set the stop-watch for one minute, and that you want them to sit very still and silent until the minute is up. (This proves to be extremely difficult for some children!) With a flourish, set the time and say 'Now!'

When the timer beeps, ask the children to think about what else they might have done in that minute – for example, touched all four walls of the classroom, walked to the Head's room and back, taken out their reading book and read a page. Use the timer to try out some of the children's suggestions and see how accurate their guesses were.

Ask the children whether they know how many seconds make up a minute. Write 60 on the flip chart. Look at a second hand on a watch, and see whether the children can clap accurately to the beat.

Now ask the children to suggest what they could do, without moving from where they are, that would take about a second: *clap my hands, stamp my foot, sneeze, smile, tap my toes, stand up, sit down* and so on. Test their guesses using the timer. Ask the children to try out the activities you have already planned, and check the time they take.

Organize the children into groups, and ask each group to report back with four ideas for things they can do in the classroom which take about a second: *switch on the light, find a pencil, open my reading book, untie my shoe lace, take off my jumper...* Try out the ideas against the clock when they report back.

The groups can follow this up by using the percussion instruments to see what actions take one second: *beating the drum, shaking the bells, rattling the tambourine...* They can practise keeping time with a steady percussion beat.

Read out the poem 'In one second' (photocopiable page 137), and look at the enlarged copy of the poem together. Demonstrate on the flip chart how the children can write a similar poem by substituting their own ideas. Scribe a list of the children's ideas, making a pattern:

> In one second
> I can
> twiddle my thumbs,
> stretch out my arms,
> smile at my friend.
>
> In one second
> I can
> open my book,
> write the date,
> draw a straight line.

Now demonstrate how a poem can be made from the children's exploration of keeping time on percussion instruments – for example:

In one second
I can
bang my drum,
rattle my tambourine,
shake my bells.

Encourage the children to create verses which refer to different places (the classroom, the kitchen, the playground and so on), using three linked ideas for each place:

In one second
I can
turn on the tap,
splash my jumper,
spill water on the floor!

Write a few of the children's 'In one second' verses on the flip chart. Divide the class into the appropriate number of groups and read the verses on the flip chart as a round. Add the line *In one second* to the end of each verse and let the readings overlap slightly, so that as one group is reading the last line another group is starting with the same line.

Finally, give out copies of photocopiable page 138. Ask the children to fill in the missing lines, creating their own 'In one second' poems. The writing frame follows the pattern which has been established on the flip chart. There should be a reading and sharing time for all those who would like to read their work aloud.

Suggestion(s) for extension

Children who are independent writers can adapt the pattern to make list poems which refer to other people – for example:

In one second
my baby brother can
spill his milk,
throw custard on the floor,
smile at my mum.

In one second
my dad can
hammer a nail,
bash his thumb,
shout very loud!

Suggestion(s) for support

Help those children who need support to read the enlarged poem aloud. Point out what is the same in all three verses, and what is different.

Assessment opportunities

Look for those children who can make appropriate substitutions, and who understand how time is measured. Note those who need help with adapting the pattern.

Opportunities for IT

The children could use an art package to create pictures of a candle clock, an egg timer, a stopwatch, a grandfather clock and so on. These could also be taken from clip art collections or scanned from the children's own line drawings. They could type their verse of the poem into a space next to their picture in the art package; or the pictures could be added to word-processed versions of their poems (or used as a background for the text).

A more ambitious project would be to make an electronic presentation of the poems using multimedia authoring software. The children can use their clock pictures (see above) and the text of their verses. Each page of the presentation could be one child's verse, with the pictures and text arranged in frames on the page. They could add sounds recorded with a microphone attached to the computer: clocks ticking, percussion instruments playing or the children reading their verses for the poem.

The presentation could start with a title page on which each of the authors' names is shown. Each name is then linked to that child's page, which contains the poem, pictures and sound effects. Buttons or icons on the page could allow the sound effects to be played. Backwards and forwards arrow buttons will take the reader on to the next page, or back to the first page. Figure 2 shows an example.

The presentation could also be set up to scroll through each verse in turn – an ideal arrangement for a parents' evening! It is usually a good idea for you to set up the structure of the presentation in advance and show groups of children how to create their own page. Such work often needs the support of another adult helper, especially when the children are new to the ideas.

In one second

July 14th

I can
open my book
write the date
draw a straight line

Figure 2

Display ideas

The children can cut out pictures and photographs of clocks and watches from old catalogues and advertisements. These can be stuck collage-style on backing paper, around the children's poems.

Reference to photocopiable sheets

Photocopiable page 137 should be copied onto an A3 sheet or OHT for display during the lesson. Photocopiable page 138 is a writing frame adapted from the poem on page 137; the children should fill in the gaps with their own ideas.

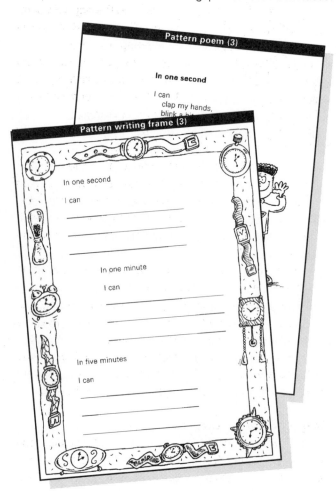

FIVE SENSES

To create a class poem based on the pattern of a published poem, carefully selecting descriptive language. To read their own poems aloud, and to compare them with the original poem.

†† *Whole class, five groups.*

⏲ *50 minutes.*

⚠ *Make sure that appropriate hygiene procedures are observed if food is to be handled or eaten. Be aware of any possible food allergies or dietary restrictions.*

Previous skills/knowledge needed

It would be helpful, but is not essential, for the children to know that they have five senses, and to be able to define them. They should be ready to listen and respond to poems and stories read aloud.

Key background knowledge

This activity is based on the idea of favourite sensations. Be ready to explore the children's likes and dislikes, channelling their suggestions into lines which echo the beat of the original poem. Encourage the children to relate their contributions to the ongoing discussion, taking other children's views into account, so that a productive dialogue ensues. This activity can be linked to a science topic such as 'Our senses' or 'All about me'.

Preparation

Make an enlarged (A3) copy or OHT of photocopiable page 139. Make some copies of photocopiable page 140 (see 'Suggestion(s) for support'). Provide some books suitable for topic work on the senses. Gather a collection of objects for the children to explore with their senses, taking shape and colour, texture, smell and possibly taste into account (fresh fruit is suitable for all these categories). Gather a number of objects which can be used to make different sounds – percussion instruments are perhaps the easiest to find. The objects should be kept hidden in a bag or box until they are needed.

Resources needed

A range of objects to stimulate discussion on the senses (see above), books relevant to topic work on the senses, a flip chart, writing materials, photocopiable pages 139 and 140.

What to do

Arrange the children in a semicircle around you for comfortable listening, ideally in the story corner. Initiate a discussion on their senses by telling them that they are going to be detectives. You have some secret objects hidden in the box, and they must try to find out what these objects are without looking. *How can you find out what is in the box? If your eyes aren't allowed to help, what will?*

Elicit that they must use their hands and fingers to detect what the objects are: they need to touch the object. Let one child have a go, touching and feeling the objects in the box. He or she might find an apple, for example. Ask whether he or she can tell the others what the secret object is. If the child says immediately that the object is an apple, ask what it felt like: *round, cold, smooth, with a little stick on the top*, and so on. Ask the children which of their senses provided the answer. Establish that *touch* is one of their senses. Scribe *touch* on the flip chart.

Use the same procedure for other fruits (for example, a banana, an orange and a pineapple), taking the opportunity to explore some of the vocabulary of touch and texture: *knobbly, rough, smooth, slippery* and so on.

Return to the apple and ask whether the children know what colour it is. They will probably try to guess – but say that they need to use another sense to find out: they need to see the apple. Tell the children that this sense is called *sight*, and scribe the word on the flip chart. Ask the children for colour words, and scribe these beneath the *sight* heading.

Ask the children to smell the fruits and tell you what they smell. Scribe any descriptive words they suggest on the flip chart under *smell* – for example, *sour, flowery* or *spicy*.

If you wish to explore taste with the children, first make sure that no child is allergic to any of the fruits you intend to use. Take the opportunity to cut up an apple and/or banana, and let those who wish to do so describe the taste. If you don't want the children to do this, simply ask what they think the taste would be like and whether they would like it or not. Scribe *taste* on the flip chart with some of the children's language (*sour, sweet, bitter, crunchy* and so on).

Let a child hide out of sight, making a sound with one of the percussion instruments. Ask the other children to guess which instrument is being played. Repeat this with another child and another instrument. Establish that this is *sound*, the fifth sense, and scribe the word on the flip chart. Again, encourage the children to suggest sound words: *loud, soft, ringing, drumming, rattling* and so on.

Go over the names of the five senses and some of the associated vocabulary, reading from the lists you have made on the flip chart. Now settle the children down and ask them to listen to a poem. Read the poem 'I like' aloud, with the children following it on the enlarged version. Ask the children which words are used a lot in the poem. The children should be able to see that the poem is made up of five two-line verses, every verse starting with the words *I like...*

Ask: *What does the poet like to taste? Who would like a different taste?* Use some of the children's ideas to make up a new first line, such as *I like the taste of sherbet sweets*. Now work with the children to construct a second line which echoes the original – for example, *I like the taste of sherbet sweets / fizzing on my tongue*. Use some of the words from the flip chart, or find new ones. Scribe the lines that the children like best.

Working either in groups or as a class, move on to look at the other verses – again, substituting the children's suggestions for those in the original poem:

▲ *I like the smell of flowers / tickling my nose.*

▲ *I like the touch of my cat's fur / silky under my hand.*

▲ *I like the sound of bells / ringing in my ears.*

▲ *I like the sight of sea-spray / sparkling in my eyes.*

Remind the children of the two-line pattern for each verse, and help them to use interesting vocabulary such as *tickling, silky, sparkling* and so on. Choose one suggested verse for each of the senses to make up a new poem, and scribe it on the flip chart.

Now divide the children into five groups and allocate a sense to each group. Read out the original poem and then the children's new version, with each group reading four lines each. Help those children whose confidence needs a boost by sharing the reading task with them.

Take a few minutes to let the children reflect on the new poem which they have created. How is it different from the original? Which do they prefer and why?

Suggestion(s) for extension

Children who are confident readers and writers could copy the sense headings from the flip chart, then list things they *don't* like to see, smell, taste, touch or listen to. Working individually or as a group, and using the original poem as a pattern, these children could make up a new 'Don't like' senses poem – for example:

The children could read or recite their 'Don't like' poem(s) to the rest of the class.

I don't like the taste of curry
burning on my tongue.

I don't like the smell of grass
making sneezes come to my nose.

I don't like the feel of a woolly scarf
all scratchy on my hand.

I don't like the sound of the alarm clock
telling my ears it's time for school.

I don't like the look of my first photographs
crying big tears from my eyes.

Suggestion(s) for support

Less able children could use photocopiable page 140, filling in new words or drawing pictures in the spaces. Talk with them about what they would like to taste, smell and so on; in particular, help them to choose an appropriate first word for each second line. They might suggest verses such as:
▲ *I like the taste of chocolate / gooey on my tongue.*
▲ *I like the smell of ginger / nippy at my nose.*
Help the children to find expressive words, even if they are slightly unconventional!

Assessment opportunities

Note those children who can follow the pattern of a poem, using substitution. Look for those who can find and use interesting describing words.

Opportunities for IT

Each child could use the word processor to add something that they like or dislike to a wall-chart. They could type in their like or dislike, then format their writing in a font or colour that they like or don't like. Where the likes and dislikes can be represented pictorially, the children could add clip art images or pictures they have drawn with an art package to illustrate their words. They will need to remember that the display must be legible from a distance.

Display ideas

The children could draw (or cut out of magazines) pictures of things they like to see, smell, touch, taste and listen to. These could be used to make a collage of the five senses, with sections headed *We like to see... We like to taste... We like to listen to...* and so on.

Reference to photocopiable sheets

Photocopiable page 139 should be copied onto an A3 sheet or OHT for display during the lesson. Children who need support can use the writing frame on photocopiable page 140, either filling in new words or drawing pictures in the spaces.

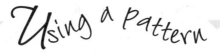

COUNTDOWN

To create a rhyming poem, using a published poem as a model.

†† *Whole class, then individual work.*

🕐 *40 minutes.*

Previous skills/knowledge needed

This activity builds on the experience the children have gained from the activity 'How many stars?' (page 51). They should be able to count down from 10 to 1; and they should be ready to share their ideas with others in the class.

Key background information

This activity is a progression from the number poem writing activity 'How many stars?' It uses many of the same teaching techniques, such as the strategy of modelling a poem on the flip chart based on the children's original ideas. The children are invited to compare and contrast their own star number poems with Jack Prelutsky's poem 'Countdown'.

Preparation

Make an enlarged (A3) copy or OHT of photocopiable page 141. Make one copy per child of photocopiable page 142. Find some number poems in anthologies or collections (for example, *One in a Million* edited by Moira Andrew, Puffin 1992).

Resources needed

Photocopiable pages 141 and 142, a flip chart, writing materials, a 1–10 number line, some published number poems.

What to do

Gather the children together with a clear view of the number line. Consolidate the children's number knowledge by reading out the numbers from 1 to 10 and back again. Talk about the countdown used before a rocket is launched, and encourage the children to join in counting ... *3, 2, 1, Zero, BLAST-OFF!* They are usually enthusiastic about this!

Tell the children that you are going to read a number poem. Read out 'Countdown' by Jack Prelutsky (photocopiable page 141) and talk about its content. *Who is the poem all about? Where do you think the ghosts are living?* (In a haunted house, a ruined castle, a spooky palace...)

Read the lines *There are two ghosts on the carpet / Doing things that ghosts will do.* Ask what these things might be. (Frightening people, saying *Whoooo!*, hiding in corners, disappearing into the air...) Let the children express their ideas about ghosts; but keep the whole discussion light, and be sensitive to any children who may be frightened by the thought of a ghost.

Using the enlarged version or OHT of photocopiable page 141, let the children look at Jack Prelutsky's poem. Encourage them to talk about it and express opinions on whether the title is appropriate and why the poet might have chosen it. Let them suggest other appropriate titles such as 'Haunted house' or 'How many ghosts?'

Read out the poem again, covering up the words. Stop just before each rhyme and ask the children to say the right word. Discuss how they knew to say *chairs, wall...* and *BOO!* at the right time.

Talk about what a rhyme is. Can they think of another rhyme for *stairs*? They may suggest *lairs, cares, dares...* Tell them that the clever trick is to make the rhyme match the content of the poem, so that it 'sounds right'. *There are seven ghosts saying their prayers* might do. Can the children think of another rhyme for *hall*? They might suggest *There are three ghosts playing ball.* The last rhyme suggests some fun possibilities: *There is one ghost right behind me... But where? I haven't a clue!* or *I'll chase you, ghost, so SHOO!* or *Hey, I didn't know ghosts were blue!* Let the children enjoy working on this kind of substitution, trading ideas orally across the class.

If the children have previously completed the activity 'How many stars?' (see page 51), encourage a few of them to read their versions of the star number poem. Encourage them to compare these with 'Countdown'. *Where is the pattern the same?* Both poems are countdowns from 10 to 1. Both poems talk about the same things in every line (stars or ghosts). *How are the poems different?* There are no describing words in Jack Prelutsky's poem, and it doesn't say what the ghosts are doing.

Use the flip chart to create a class version of 'Countdown', keeping to the haunted house or castle scenario. Take ideas from the children. They will probably suggest skeletons, spiders, bats and so on. Again, keep the fun aspect uppermost. You might scribe, for example:

There are ten skeletons in the kitchen,
There are nine hiding by the door.
[Use the original poem to point out which is the next line to have a rhyme at the end.]
There are eight skeletons in the bedroom,
There are seven dancing on the floor.
There are six skeletons in the cupboard,
There are five splashing in the bath.
There are four skeletons in the cellar.
There are three trying not to laugh.
There are two skeletons in the garden,
Rattling every bone.
There's one skeleton just behind me –
I shouldn't have come here alone!

Encourage the children to create this kind of rhyming poem orally – keeping in mind the pattern of the original, the rhyme scheme and the general feel.

Give out copies of photocopiable page 142 and let the children fill in the gaps to create their own haunted house or haunted castle 'countdown' poems, featuring the numbers of bats or spiders or moths.

Suggestion(s) for extension

Children who are independent writers could work in pairs to write a true countdown poem – for a rocket. First, they should list ten different things needed for a space launch: astronauts, scientists, space shuttles, orbits, boosters, controls, rockets... Then they should construct a simple rhyming poem – for example:

10 astronauts waving goodbye.
9 doors shutting tight.
8 scientists counting down.
7 screens blinking bright.
6 boosters revving up.
5 controls in a row.
4 rockets shuddering.
3 head-sets saying 'Go!'
2 fuel tanks in place.
1 shuttle off to space!
   Zero...
   BLAST-OFF!

Suggestion(s) for support

An adult could work with a group of less confident children, using the flip chart to scribe their ideas. They might work together in this way to create a countdown poem, using only the numbers from 5 to 1. When this group have finished and are satisfied with their poem, let them read it aloud to the other children in the class – each child reading one or two lines, depending on the size of the group.

Assessment opportunities

Note those children who can base their own work on a given pattern. Look for those who can find appropriate rhymes and use them with understanding.

Opportunities for IT

To encourage the children to originate their work using a word processor, you could create a framework or template file (based on photocopiable page 142) for them to use. The file should be saved onto disk so that the children can retrieve it, rename it and save it as their own work. This will allow the children to concentrate on the creative aspect of the work, and let them draft and redraft their poem more easily. Younger or less able children may need adult support in using the framework file.

The children's printed countdown poems, either written at the computer or typed in later, could be 'published' as a class anthology. The children could illustrate their poems, using pictures created with an art package or scanned from their own line drawings.

Display ideas

Paint a haunted house or castle background. The children can cut out ghost-like shapes from white tissue or crêpe paper; they should have no recognizable limbs, and no features except for large round eyes. The 'ghosts' can be pasted in an overlapping chain through the various rooms of the castle. (See Figure 3.) The children can add spiders, skeletons and other spooky painted or cut-out images. Scribe a version of the children's joint poem underneath the frieze.

Figure 3

Performance ideas
Ten children can dress up in sheets to represent the ghosts in Jack Prelutsky's poem 'Countdown', miming while one undisguised child nervously reads or recites the poem.

Reference to photocopiable sheets
Photocopiable page 141 should be copied onto an A3 sheet or OHT for display during the lesson. Photocopiable page 142 is a writing frame adapted from the poem on page 141; the children should fill in the gaps with their own ideas.

Pattern writing frame (5)

Countdown

There are 10 _____

There are 9 _____ in the _____

There are 8 _____ on the floor.

There are 7 _____ in the _____

There are 6 _____ behind the _____

There are 5 _____ in the _____

There are 4 _____ on the wall.

There are 3 _____ in the _____

There are 2 _____ in the _____

And one is _____ under the bed.

FOR THE FIRST TIME

To recognize a chorus in a poem. To write a poem with a chorus, using a simple poetry structure. To compare and contrast two poems on the same subject.

†† *Whole class, groups, then individual work.*

🕑 *45 minutes.*

Previous skills/knowledge needed
The children should be used to taking part in whole-class oral activities, and be ready to share some of their personal experiences with others in the class. They should be accustomed to offering ideas and suggestions for consideration by other children.

Key background information
This activity teaches children to recognize a chorus (or refrain) in a poem. Try to orchestrate the activity so that the children are happy to recount some of their own personal experiences of things that happened to them 'for the first time'. Encourage them to express excitement, surprise or disappointment as appropriate. These ideas should be incorporated into a model poem on the flip chart.

Preparation
Make an enlarged (A3) copy or OHT of photocopiable page 143. Make one copy per child of photocopiable page 144. Bring in a few brand new and obviously unused things for the children to handle (with care) – for example, a T-shirt with the label still attached, a new exercise book, an unopened packet of seeds, a new box of pencils, and so on. Find some poetry anthologies or collections which include chorus poems (see 'Suggestion(s) for extension').

Resources needed
Photocopiable pages 143 and 144, a flip chart, writing materials, a few new objects (see above), some published chorus poems.

What to do
Gather the children as a group to sit in the library corner. Read the poem 'First things' by John Cotton (see page 143) aloud. Encourage the children to think about some of the 'first things' the author writes about: licking a lolly, biting a cake, opening a new comic, swimming in the sea and so on. Ask whether they would choose the same things to be excited about. If not, what can they suggest instead?

Use the new things which you have collected to stimulate interest and discussion. For example, the children might look at the way that a new garment is uncreased and its colours are brighter than usual. They could smell a new exercise book, and imagine how the seeds in a packet will look when the flowers come up.

Encourage the children to explore their own memories of things that they have enjoyed doing for the first time. For example, they might recall travelling in an aeroplane, wearing new trainers, feeling snow underfoot in winter, feeling sand underfoot on holiday... Scribe some of these ideas under headings: *wearing, feeling, tasting, playing* and so on. Suggest that the children try to imagine they have never done any of these things before. How would they feel? – *excited, thrilled, pleased, surprised* and so on.

From the children's ideas, invent a suitable scenario. Scribe an opening line on the flip chart – for example:

I went down to the sea

Add a chorus line:

for the first time, for the first time.

Ask the children to imagine seeing the sea for the first time. *Imagine how exciting it would be. What would you see?* Sand, cliffs, beach umbrellas, children... *What would you hear?* Seagulls, waves, children calling... *What would the sand and the rocks feel like?* and so on.

Suggest that the children explore some of these ideas through their senses – for example: *I saw gulls wheel through the sky, I saw children playing on the sand... I heard waves splash on the shore, I heard gulls scream in the air... I felt waves tickle my feet, I felt the sand burning my toes...* Show how you can put some of these ideas together to start a poem that has a chorus:

I went down to the sea
for the first time, for the first time.
I felt waves tickle my feet
for the first time, for the first time.
  I went down to the sea
  for the first time, for the first time.
  I saw gulls wheel through the sky
  for the first time, for the first time.
    I went down to the sea
    for the first time, for the first time.
    I heard waves splashing on rocks
    for the first time, for the first time.

The trick is to give the poem a rhythmic beat. For example, in the first line, it is possible to say *shore* instead of *sea*, but *seashore* would not fit – it has too many syllables. In the same way, *I heard the sea splashing on the rocks* doesn't sound right, but *I heard waves splashing on rocks* fits perfectly. Scribe the children's ideas, but alter them to make them rhythmic if necessary.

Read out the first and third lines of the model poem on the flip chart, asking the children to respond each time with *for the first time, for the first time.* Tell them that this is called the **chorus**. Divide the class into groups and have each group read out the model poem, with the rest of the class joining in the chorus.

Now try writing shared poems about other new scenarios: *I travelled by plane, We climbed up a mountain, I helped in the kitchen, We went to the shops, I saw my new brother, I went to a Villa match,* and so on. Keep the beat going, with everyone joining in the chorus lines. Ask the children to suggest an appropriate third line for each new poem; these lines should begin *I/We saw... I/We heard... I/We felt...* Make this a quick-fire oral game, with ideas coming thick and fast.

Scribe three or four of the most popular first lines on the flip chart. Give out copies of photocopiable page 144. Ask the children to make up their own chorus poems by filling in the blanks on the sheet. They can take their first line from the flip chart, or invent one of their own.

To conclude the activity, read out the poem 'First things' again. Display the enlarged copy of the poem (photocopiable page 143). Compare it with one of the class poems on the flip chart, or one of the poems that the children have written on their copies of photocopiable page 144. *What is the same?* (They all describe 'first things'.) *What is different?* ('First things' rhymes and 'For the first time' doesn't. John Cotton's poem has no chorus and 'For the first time' has a chorus.)

Suggestion(s) for extension
Children who are independent writers could add an extra line to their poems:

I went down to the sea
for the first time, for the first time.
I heard seas splashing on rocks
  like waterfalls crashing *or* like hoses gushing
or like cold taps in the bath *or* like the rain pouring down
for the first time, for the first time.

I met my new baby brother
for the first time, for the first time.
I heard him crying for my mum
  like a kitten meowing *or* like a seabird calling
or like an alarm going off
for the first time, for the first time.

strawberries, pizzas and so on, showing one big bite taken out of each item. The pictures can be stuck collage-style on a dark-coloured backing sheet, with the title 'The first bite'.

Performance ideas
The children can role-play their 'first time' at the sea, at the shops, on a mountain and so on, following some of the poems modelled on the flip chart. One child can read each poem and they can all join in the chorus, trying to make each 'for the first time' sound different (said softly, in a strong voice, mysteriously and so on).

Reference to photocopiable sheets
Photocopiable page 143 should be copied onto an A3 sheet or OHT for display during the lesson. Photocopiable page 144 is a writing frame which the children can use to create a chorus poem, similar in theme to the poem on page 143 but different in style.

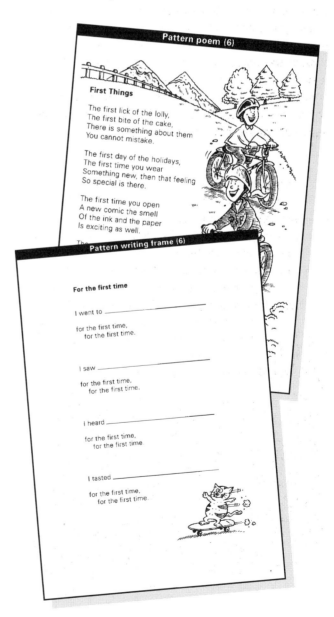

Let these children look through collections and anthologies of poetry to find examples of chorus poems. They should mark them with Post-it Notes and read their favourites aloud to the others.

Suggestion(s) for support
Less able children could be supported by having an adult helper to scribe their ideas for a collaborative group poem. They could read the poem aloud to the rest of the class, with everyone joining in the chorus.

Assessment opportunities
Note those children who can recognize a chorus or refrain, and those who can use a simple structure to create their own poems. Look for those who have the vocabulary needed to compare and contrast two poems.

Opportunities for IT
You could create a template writing frame on the word processor for some children to use in originating and editing their poems. They could be shown how to 'cut and paste' the line *for the first time, for the first time,* instead of retyping it. For the youngest or least confident writers, the whole poem structure could be included in the file. More independent writers could extend the framework file, adding extra lines where they need them.

Display ideas
The children can paint and cut out pictures of things they would like to eat, such as apples, cakes, biscuits,

WHEN THE WIND BLOWS

To use a simple, repetitive poetry pattern to compose their own poems through substitution.

†† *Whole class, then individual work.*

🕐 *50 minutes.*

Previous skills/knowledge needed

The children should be used to listening to poems and stories being read aloud, and to sharing their thoughts and ideas with others in the group. They should be aware of different kinds of weather, and the clothes and activities appropriate to each kind.

Key background information

This activity is based on a simple, repetitive poetry structure. The text provided should be used first for shared reading, then as a basis for shared writing, and finally as a pattern for individual writing. Show the children that you enjoy the *wordsearch* involved in shared writing, and encourage them to trade words and ideas in order to arrive at an exciting use of language.

Preparation

Make an enlarged (A3) copy or OHT of photocopiable page 145. Make one copy per child of photocopiable page 146. Gather together a few weather props – for example, a bobble hat and scarf for a windy day, boots and an umbrella for rain, sunglasses and a sun-hat for a bright day.

Resources needed

Photocopiable pages 145 and 146, some weather props (as above), a flip chart, writing materials, wax crayons or coloured pencils.

What to do

Gather the children together, sitting in a place where the flip chart and enlarged poem will be clearly visible to everyone. Introduce the activity by talking about today's weather. *Can you remember what the weather was like yesterday?* Talk with the children about the particular clothes people might wear, the sounds they might hear and the way they would feel on a very hot day, in the rain, on a windy day and so on. Take time to let the children exchange views on the weather and how it changes things around them. Produce your collection of weather props and ask a child to pick out something suitable for a sunny day. Ask

why he or she has chosen the sun-hat or sunglasses. Work in a similar way with the rainy or windy day props, making sure that the children offer a reason for their choice: *to keep the sun off, to keep you dry, to keep you warm,* and so on.

Tell the children that you want to show them a poem about a windy day. Display the enlarged version of 'When the wind blows' (photocopiable page 145); say that you are going to read it to them, and then they can join in a second reading. Read it through and allow the usual thinking time. Before the children read the poem aloud, ask whether anyone can make a comment about the way the poem is written (for example, *It has a pattern of pairs of lines, except at the end. Every first line is the same.*) Establish that the children know that each set of lines makes a **verse**, so the poem has six verses. Ask what words each verse begins with.

Make the reading a shared experience, perhaps dividing the class into groups to read the second line of each verse and saying *When the wind blows* all together as a chorus. Find different ways of expressing the chorus line – for example, starting almost as a whisper and building up to a crescendo. (See 'Performance ideas'.)

Look now at what the poem is describing: things we wear, things outside, things indoors. Ask the children to think about the last verse, and establish that they have some understanding of the word *haven* and the contrast it makes with the idea of *a battle*. Explore the possible reasons for the poet using these words: *It's quiet inside, but outside it's noisy... It's safe inside, but outside it's dangerous...* and so on. Emphasize the neat way he has rounded off the poem by showing a contrast between indoors and outdoors. Read the poem aloud again.

Turn to the flip chart and scribe *When the wind blows.* Explore with the children the idea of writing 'copycat' poems for other kinds of weather. What would their first line look like for snow, rain, sun or fog? Perhaps they could choose between *When the snow falls* and *When the sun shines.* Take one of the ideas and scribe a model poem on the flip chart, following the pattern of the original poem as closely as you can. Start by thinking about clothes; then perhaps the garden, the school, the park and the beach; finish off with an inside-outside contrast. For example:

When the sun shines
Shady hats, no shoes.
or Jumpers off, bathers on.

When the sun shines
Flowers open, apples ripen.
or Roses grow, grass fades.

When the sun shines
Babies cry, cats sleep.
or Dads snooze, children play.

When the sun shines
Water sparkles, shadows dance.
or Waves whisper, sand burns.

When the sun shines
Outside is hot, inside is cool.
or Outside glares, inside dims.

When the fog drifts
Coats are buttoned up.

When the fog drifts
Trees disappear, fences fade.

When the fog drifts
Cars slow, lorries brake.

When the fog drifts
Leaves sag, flowers die.

When the fog drifts
Indoors it's bright,
Outside it's dark.

Encourage the children to share their finished work with their classmates.

There are lots of possibilities; but with the children's help, search for the lines that you think can make the most of the pattern John Foster has set. Let the children see you using drafting procedures: crossing out and replacing words, reading the poem aloud to adjust the rhythm, and so on. Explain what you are doing each time, so that the children can model their writing on this shared activity.

Give out copies of photocopiable page 146. Encourage the children to write their own ideas on the blank lines, following the pattern of the original poem. They can illustrate their finished work with wax crayons or coloured pencils. Finally, let some of the children read their poems aloud.

Suggestion(s) for extension

Children who are independent writers could choose another kind of weather as the subject for a new poem, following the pattern of the original. For example, they might tackle 'When the rain falls', 'When the fog drifts' or 'When the frost comes'. Suggest that they start with clothes and move on to a suitable place (the garden or, in the case of fog, the roads), thinking about the problems that kind of weather can bring. For example:

Suggestion(s) for support

Children who need support could follow the main pattern of the poem by starting each set of two lines with the words *When the sun shines*, but adopting a simpler model for the second line of each verse. A supportive adult should ask *When the sun shines, what do you wear?* and elicit responses such as *We wear sun-hats, caps with peaks, sun-glasses, shorts, T-shirts...* Working either as a group or individually, the children should write a second line such as: *When the sun shines / We wear our T-shirts.*

This is a more natural sentence (and is thus easier to write) than in the original pattern. The adult can go on to ask similar questions: *When the sun shines, where do you like to go? What do you like to do? What do parents do?* and so on. The poem will begin to look like this:

When the sun shines
We wear our T-shirts.
When the sun shines
We go to the beach.
When the sun shines
We splash in the sea... and so on.

The children should share their finished poems with the rest of the class.

Assessment opportunities

Note those children who can follow the pattern of the original poem. Look for those who are able and willing to share and modify their ideas.

Opportunities for IT

You could create a template writing frame on the word processor, for some children to use in originating and editing their poems. More independent writers could extend the

framework file, adding extra lines where they need them. They could be shown how to use the 'search and replace' facility to change all the *When the sun shines* lines to a different type of weather.

The children's finished poems could be word-processed and presented in a large text style, for use in a class display on different types of weather.

Display ideas

Paint four panels, each showing a different kind of weather, and display the children's poems on the appropriate panels. Place a table beneath the paintings to display some of the weather props, as well as some illustrated books and poems about weather. Above the paintings, display an enlarged copy of John Foster's poem pasted onto a dark backing sheet.

Performance ideas

The children can practise reciting the poem 'When the wind blows', with everyone joining in the repeated line and individuals or small groups saying the other lines. The children should explore different ways of expressing the chorus line (see 'What to do'), and make the whole performance as dramatic as possible. This performance would be a useful part of a topic on weather.

Reference to photocopiable sheets

The poem on photocopiable page 145 should be copied onto an A3 sheet or OHT for display during the lesson. Photocopiable page 146 is a writing frame which encourages the children to use the pattern of the original poem to write about several kinds of weather, adding their own ideas to the blank lines.

MY HOME

To write poems based on the structure of a humorous poem, paying particular attention to rhyme and rhythm.

†† *Whole class.*

🕐 *50 minutes.*

Previous skills/knowledge needed

The children need to have experience of listening to nursery rhymes and rhyming poems. They should have developed a good ear for rhyme, and be used to following a poetry pattern through shared writing. They should also be used to group listening, and be prepared to share their ideas and comments with others in the class.

Key background information

This activity moves the children on from listening to traditional nursery rhymes (as in 'Number rhymes', page 23) to hearing and creating rhymes which describe everyday modern objects in rhythmic, rhyming language. The work involved will help the children to develop their skills in using rhyme, and to relate this experience to spelling patterns by generating 'strings' or 'families' of rhyming words in written form.

From their experience of shared writing, the children should be confident about using substitution to create their own poems based on the pattern of Colin West's poem. Despite its serious intentions, this activity should be a lot of fun for the children who take part.

Preparation

Make an enlarged (A3) copy or OHT of photocopiable page 147. Read this poem before starting the activity, and collect some of the items mentioned in the poem (a pebble, a paper clip, a lollipop and so on). Collect some other everyday 'starters' to stimulate the children's writing (see 'Suggestion(s) for extension'), such as a pencil, ball, apple, umbrella, cap and so on.

Resources needed

Some of the items mentioned in the poem (see photocopiable page 147), some other everyday 'starters' (see 'Preparation'), a flip chart; writing materials (see 'Suggestion(s) for extension').

What to do

Gather the children together in the story corner. Introduce Colin West's poem 'Home' by showing the children a box of paper clips. Ask: *Do you know what these are called? What are they used for?* Discuss with the children where they might find paper clips: in their desks, on the floor, in their mother's briefcase and so on. Look at a towel, asking where these are usually found: in the bathroom, by the kitchen sink, on a towel rail, and so on.

Tell the children that you have a poem about where different things 'live'. Read 'Home' (photocopiable page 147) and leave the usual minute or two of thinking time. Then ask about the pebble in the poem: *Where is the pebble's home?* Ask where else you might find a pebble: on the beach, in the sea, in the garden and so on.

Show the children the enlarged copy of 'Home'. Read it through again, pointing out words and phrases as you come to them. Let the children read it aloud with you. Remind them that each group of four lines is called a **verse**. Count the number of verses in the poem.

Establish with the children that every verse begins with the same words: *I am a...* Ask them who (or what) is speaking in the first verse. Read with them, *I am a pebble...* Ask the children to find all the things that 'speak' in the poem: pebble, paper clip, lollipop, towel, number, kite.

Ask the children what other words appear in every verse: *My home is...* Discuss this theme with the class, and encourage them to relate these repeated words to the poem's title.

Let the children look for rhyming words in the first verse: *red/bed*. Encourage them to find more words to rhyme with red: *said, fed, led, dead, head...* Help them to make up a new first verse by creating several versions which move gradually away from the original. For example:

I am a pebble
Shiny red,
My home is on
The garden bed.
   I am a pebble
   Shiny red,
   'My home's on the beach,'
   The pebble said.
      I am a pebble
      Smooth and red,
      My home is under
      The garden shed.
         I am a pebble
         Smooth and grey,
         My home is the park
         Where children play.

Use a similar technique with the other verses. You may wish to show the children some of the actual objects in the poem; this is not essential, but may be useful in holding the concentration of less focused children. First gather a set of rhyming words to match the second line of the verse, and see whether these can be used to keep the pattern going: *clip... slip, drip, chip, ship; lollipop... shop, drop, stop, mop; pink... sink, drink, link; four... door, store, more, floor; hues... choose, lose, blues.* Possible new verses might include:

I am a silver
Paper clip,
My home's on the floor
So please don't slip.
   I am an orange
   Lollipop,
   My home is in
   The corner shop.

Work orally with the children on these verses. You may find that it is not always possible to come up with a matching rhyme that makes sense; if so, change the second line of the verse to a different rhyme (for example, *With stripes of pink* could become *With stripes of green* or *With purple dots*). Try to make each verse rhyme, scan and make sense, while keeping to the original pattern (*I am a...* and *My home is...*) In the example below, *Of many hues* is lost and a new idea creeps in:

I am a kite
And I can fly.
My home is in
The bright blue sky.

Encourage the children to trade ideas until they have a verse that sounds more or less right. Scribe the most successful, interesting or humorous verses and read them aloud as a new poem, with the children joining in.

Suggestion(s) for extension

Children who are confident about writing independently could create their own poem using new 'starters'. Reinforce the pattern orally: *I am a... / [description] / My home is... / [matching rhyme on the last line]*.

If a child chooses to write about a pencil, for example, ask him or her to suggest a good home for it. Let the children see that the home must fit the thing they have chosen to write about. Thus a ball might have a home *in the sky, over the garden wall, in the goal net*, and so on. They might write:

I am a pencil
Sharp and slim.
My home is in
The classroom bin.
I am a pencil
Red as your face,
My home is in
Tom's pencil case.
I am a pencil
Sharp I'll stay.
My home is in
Your tidy tray.

or I am a ball
Red and round,
My home is where
I can't be found!
I am a blue
And yellow ball
My home is over
The garden wall.

They could go on to look at creatures and their homes – for example:

I am a blackbird
Wild and free,
My home is in
The apple tree.
I am a dark-coated
velvet mole,
My home is in
A deep dark hole.

I am a frisbee.
I spin up high.
My home is in
The sunny sky.
My home is where
I like to fly.
My home is where
The clouds go by.

Assessment opportunities

Note those children who can adapt the original structure for their own writing. Look for those who can find and use appropriate rhymes.

Opportunities for IT

The children could make a collection of rhyme lists using the word processor, and present them for display in the classroom. The rhyme lists could then be used to help children originate their own poems on the computer, perhaps using a framework file to speed up the writing process.

Display ideas

Write out the class poem on a large sheet of paper. Ask the children to illustrate it, making cameo pictures in coloured pencil or felt-tipped pen to stick round the edges of the poem.

Performance ideas

The children can wear minimal masks to represent the objects (a towel, a lollipop, a kite and so on), or hold the appropriate items one by one, as they recite the verses of the class poem (each verse is written in the first person).

Reference to photocopiable sheet

Photocopiable page 147 should be copied onto an A3 sheet or OHT for display during the lesson.

Because this creative writing activity is relatively open-ended, no writing frame photocopiable sheet is provided.

Suggestion(s) for support

Children who are struggling to find rhyming words could be encouraged to make up a list of rhyming words to go with a new idea, such as *I am a frisbee...* They can thus create a group poem which follows the basic pattern of the original poem, but uses only the *I am a...* and *My home is...* parts.

Work with the group to build a list from an initial couplet – for example: *I am a frisbee / I spin up high... fly, dry, sky, my, by, sigh, eye.* Let them cross off inappropriate words and concentrate on those that could make sense: *fly, by* and *sky* are the most likely. Encourage the children to work together on the lines which follow, until a simple patterned poem emerges – for example:

Pattern poem (8)

Home

I am a pebble
Shiny red,
My home is on
The river bed.

I am a silver
Paper clip,
My home is on
A memo slip.

I am a yellow
Lollipop,
My home is in
The village shop.

I am a towel
With stripes of pink,
My home is by
The kitchen sink.

I am a golden
Twenty-four,
My home is on
An oaken door.

I am a kite
Of many hues,
My home is where
The wind should choose.

by Colin West

Playing with forms

When you give children the opportunity to work on – or to play with – different forms of poetry, you are opening avenues of learning and enjoyment for them. Each poetic form has its own value and significance. Once you have modelled a new technique and guided the children through it, they can practise it for themselves and use your model as a reference point.

Shared and guided writing activities are an ideal way of introducing children to different forms of poetry. Encourage recognition of each form as you work on it with the children, and let them choose favourite poems in each genre to build class anthologies.

Many of the suggestions in this chapter are more word games or puzzles than poems; but they provide an excellent way of giving children confidence in the use of language. Alphabet poems, acrostics and riddles offer the children a framework within which they can set their work, moving step by step towards a finished poem. Even the most reluctant writers enjoy the challenge which these forms provide.

Key Stage 1 children often respond eagerly to the idea of working to a format. They feel a certain security in the formality of, for example, producing an acrostic. If you vary the task, encouraging the exploration of different forms, the children's work will reflect this variety; and the children will feel that they are going through a new and different writing experience each time.

 ACROSTICS

To recognize and use the acrostic form in simple poems.

†† *Whole class, pairs, then individual work.*

🕐 *40 minutes.*

Previous skills/knowledge needed

The children need to be able to spell most high-frequency words and be familiar with 'key phonic' (initial sounds) if they are to cope in any meaningful way with this activity. They should have a reasonably wide vocabulary. They should be able to identify and describe the essential characteristics of the subject of an acrostic poem.

Key background information

An acrostic is more a word game than a true poetic form. It is a kind of 'coded message' in which the name of the poem's subject is written downwards to make the first letter of each line. This activity is not an easy option for young children, and requires more skill with words than may at first appear. However, it appeals to those who enjoy solving word-puzzles, and encourages them to search their vocabulary for words that begin with the correct letter and make sense in the context of the poem.

Preparation

Make one copy per child of photocopiable page 148. Collect some pictures and posters of animals and/or plants which exemplify the seasons. It is worth spending a few minutes

working on a draft one-word acrostic – for example, 'HOLIDAY', 'CHRISTMAS' or 'SEPTEMBER'.

Resources needed

Photocopiable page 148, pictures and posters (see 'Preparation'), an alphabet frieze, a flip chart, writing materials, coloured pencils or wax crayons.

What to do

Gather the children together in a comfortable sitting position where they can all see the pictures and the flip chart. Tell them that you are going to work on a spelling game which will lead to a special kind of poem. Introduce the word **acrostic**, and explain that the title of an acrostic poem is written downwards on the left-hand side of the page, within the poem, instead of across the top.

Take the word 'HOLIDAY' as an example. Write it down the left-hand side of the flip chart, using capital letters. Tell the children that, with their help, you are going to write an acrostic poem using the letters in this word.

Start by making a 'shopping list' of ideas for the poem. Ask the children to suggest words that go with a holiday and begin with 'h' – for example, *harbour, hammock, hills, hamper, heat...* Do the same with 'o', which is more difficult: *outdoors, ocean, outside, oranges...* Make a list of a few words for each of the letters in 'holiday'.

Now show the children how to create a simple acrostic with one word per line. Remember that the words must be appropriate to the subject! The 'HOLIDAY' acrostic might look like this:

H arbour
O utdoors
L ollies
I ce-cream
D olphins
A dventure
Y achts
S easide

It is often easier to use a phrase rather than a single word; so explore the 'HOLIDAY' acrostic again, this time extending each line – for example:

H ot days	**H** ampers filled with
O ut in the sunshine,	**O** ranges and apples,
L icking lollies and	**L** emon lollies and
I ce-cream cones,	**I** ce-cream, biscuits and
D reaming of	**D** rinks, doughnuts and
A dventures on	**A** ll kinds of
Y achts with coloured	**Y** ummy things for
S ails, skimming across the sea.	**S** crumptious picnics.

Ask the children to work in pairs on their own holiday acrostic using different words and phrases from the 'shopping lists' on the flip chart, or others that they have thought of. Give them about five minutes to complete this task. Ask a few of the children who have used their own original ideas to read their work aloud to the class. Remind them that this kind of poem is called an 'acrostic'.

Show the children some of the seasonal pictures, and discuss the distinctive features of each. Using the same technique as above, model four simple one-word acrostics on the flip chart: one for each season. For example:

S unshine	**W** hite
U mbrellas	**I** ce
M oon-daisies	**N** orth Pole
M arigolds	**T** wigs
E nergy	**E** vergreen
R oses	**R** obins

Allow the occasional double word, as in 'North Pole'. One-word acrostics of this kind allow the children to use the names of colours, sounds, feelings and other things which have only a tenuous connection with the subject.

Through shared writing on the flip chart, work on acrostics which use a phrase for each line. Remind the children that the lines must describe something about the subject. Show an animal picture, such as a lion or a cat. Encourage the children to think of some characteristics of the animals: *Cats stare a lot. Cats like to sleep in the sun. Lions catch animals to eat. Lions live in Africa...* Work these ideas into acrostic poems:

L ying silently	**C** urled up
I n the long grass,	**A** sleep in
O n the alert,	**T** he summer
N ot really	**S** un.
S leeping.	

Using the same shared writing techniques, try writing acrostics for *butterfly, moth, snail, beetle, dragonfly,* and

so on. For example, words and phrases to describe a butterfly might include *beautiful patterned wings, floating and fluttering, flying in the air, very light, likes flowers, you see them in summer, they used to be caterpillars* and so on. Some of these observations will fit the acrostic pattern and others will have to be altered; this is where language skill is required.

Another possible way of presenting an acrostic is to say *B is for...* and so on – for example:

B is for beautiful wings,
U is for up in the air,
T is for travelling to the sky,
T is for treading on flowers,
E is for easy on the eye,
R is for rainbow colours,
F is for floating and fluttering,
L is for lightness of step,
Y is for yesterday's caterpillars.

To conclude the activity, give out copies of photocopiable page 148. Encourage the children to make up acrostic poems to fit the words given on the sheet. They can decorate the initial letters like an illuminated manuscript (see Figure 1).

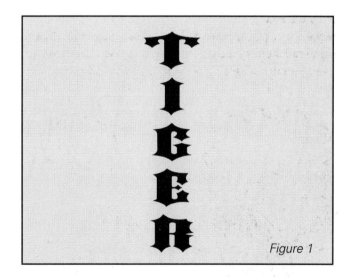

Figure 1

Suggestion(s) for extension

Children who are independent writers could work on creating one-word acrostics. They could use a dictionary to access suitable words for acrostics of calendar festivals, such as EASTER, DIVALI, TWELFTH NIGHT, CANDLEMASS [2 February] and so on. This task is not as easy as it looks!

As a further extension activity, ask more confident children to work in pairs, making acrostics of each other's names. They should exemplify some of the characteristics of their partner, including likes and dislikes. Stress that these poems should be fun: not realistic description, but not unkind. For example:

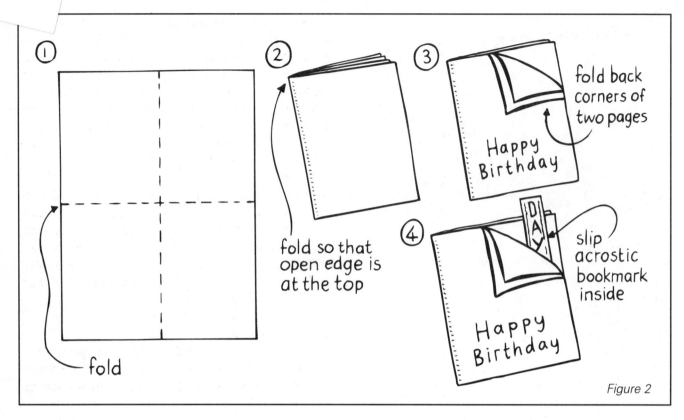

fold

② fold so that open edge is at the top

③ fold back corners of two pages

Happy Birthday

④ slip acrostic bookmark inside

Happy Birthday

Figure 2

E mily likes
M ushrooms and mangoes
I ce-cream and ice-lollies
L emon meringue pie
Y um, yum!

A ndrew hates
N ights indoors
D oing homework
R eading boring books
E verything except
W hen it's football!

F ish swim
I n the
S ea, diving
H appily.

or

F ish have dark
I nky eyes and
S ilver scales. They
H ave fins too.

Some of these acrostics could be read aloud to the class, with each child reading the acrostic which describes his or her partner.

Suggestion(s) for support

Work through photocopiable page 148 with children who need support, showing them where there is an easy word to find. In *'DOGS'*, for example, the *O* could be used for *On* or *Over* or *Out* – so ask the children what dogs sometimes like to do. *They like to run and play, chase a ball, eat their dog biscuits, sleep, bark...* Show the children how to use some of these ideas – for example:

D ogs chase the ball
O ver flowers in the
G arden and it makes dad
S hout 'Bad dog!'

or

D ogs play
O n the
G rass and bark
S ometimes.

Go through the same procedure for *'FISH'*, pointing out that the children can start with the word *Fish* and use the *I* for *In* or *Into* or even *Inky*. Showing the children an easy starting point will give them confidence to tackle the task for themselves, producing poems such as:

Assessment opportunities

Note those children who can use not only language skills but knowledge of spelling to complete this activity successfully. Children whose grasp of phonics is poor will be readily identifiable.

Opportunities for IT

The children could use a word processor to originate or present their acrostic poems. They could highlight the initial letter of each line, using a different font, a larger text size or a different colour to make it stand out (as in Figure 3). The finished acrostics could be bound together to make a class anthology, or presented in larger print for a wall display. Of course, using IT makes it possible to do either of these quite quickly. Remind the children to save their work!

E mily likes
M ushrooms and mangoes
I ce cream and ice-lollies
L emon meringue pies
Y um yum!

Figure 3

Acrostics writing frame

Key background information

'ABC poems' (or alphabet poems) are like acrostic poems (see page 90): the letters of the alphabet, in sequence, provide the first letter of each line. This activity is a good way of encouraging children to learn the sequence of letters in the alphabet, and to make use of a dictionary. Be ready to help with the more difficult letters (*x* and *z* in particular), and even to allow some cheating!

Preparation

Find some alphabet books, and some recipe books with recipes for sweets. Find some reference books which give lists of names, flowers, animals, towns, jobs people do and so on, so that you are ready to help before the children become too frustrated. Make an enlarged (A3) copy or OHT of photocopiable page 149. Make one copy per child of photocopiable page 150.

Resources needed

Photocopiable pages 149 and 150, recipe books (see above), alphabet books, an alphabet wall chart, reference books (for names, flowers, animals and so on), a flip chart, writing materials.

Display ideas

The narrow shape of an acrostic poem makes it ideal for use as a bookmark. The children can use thin card to make bookmarks as small gifts for Mother's Day, birthdays, Christmas, Divali and so on. The bookmark can be placed in the pocket of a corner card, which can be made from a square of card and folded as shown in Figure 2. The children can decorate their acrostic poems by using an illustrated script for the initial letters, as in Figure 1.

Reference to photocopiable sheet

Photocopiable page 148 provides the initial letters of three short acrostic poems. This starting-point can be given to the children for independent use; children who need support can work on the sheet with the teacher.

What to do

Gather the children together where they can sit in comfort, and where the flip chart can be easily seen by everyone. Show them an alphabet chart and recite the alphabet together. Point to each letter in turn, and make sure that all the children can match the letter shapes to the sounds.

Write the alphabet in capital letters on the flip chart, as a downwards list. You may need two columns for this. Leave enough space on the left-hand side to add an adjective later on. Establish that you have written the alphabet, and ask the children to count the number of letters aloud.

An alphabet poem using names is perhaps the easiest place to start. Look for any children whose names begin with A. Choose one of the *A* names to write on the flip chart (telling the other *A* children that they can use their names in their own poems). Fill up the alphabet list with the names of children in the class, as far as possible; then fill in the spaces with other names. You might have a list which starts like this:

> Abdi
> Ben
> Charlie
> Deema

Now ask the children to find words to describe the people on the list – but these words must begin with the same letter as the name. Choose some describing words beginning with *a*, such as *angry, amiable, affectionate,*

ABC POEMS

To use the structure of the alphabet as a starting-point for writing a poem.

†† *Whole class, groups, then individual work.*

🕐 *45 minutes.*

Previous skills/knowledge needed

The children need to have some knowledge of the alphabet and its sequence. They should be able to recognize and name individual letters. They should be used to listening to poems read aloud and sharing their ideas with others in the class.

amazing... Then go on to *b, c, d, e* and so on. Make this a quick-fire part of the activity, dealing with as many different suggestions as you can. If the children are not sure of the meaning of an unusual word, either go over it or note it for later. This exercise is ideal for extending the children's vocabulary.

Your poem on the flip chart will have grown to look like this:

Angry Abdi	Naughty Nicholas
Bashful Ben	Old-fashioned Olive
Cheerful Charlie	Popular Peter
Dotty Deema	Quiet Queenie
Energetic Edward	Rocky Ravi
Fiery Ferhana	Smiling Sarah
Generous George	Tearful Tracey
Happy Hanif	Unique Ursula
Impatient Ian	Violet Vera
Jolly Jeremy	Witty William
Kookie Kate	Xpert Xania
Lazy Lenny	Youthful Yasmin
Merry Margaret	Zestful Zena

You will note that credibility is stretched for *X* – accept *Xciting, Xcellent* and so on. It is important to keep the children's attention by maintaining the pace until the poem is finished.

Now suggest to the children that they might help you write another alphabet poem, this time using the names of sweets. Ask for their help in suggesting sweets beginning

with *a* (such as *acid drops, aniseed balls*); then *b* (*blackjacks, bulls' eyes*); *c* (*chocolate drops, coconut ice, candyfloss*); and so on. If necessary, they can use the recipe books to find ideas.

With the children's help, scribe an alphabet poem of sweets – a subject close to their hearts! The poem could look like this:

ABC of sweets
Acid drops and blackjacks,
Candyfloss and dolly mixtures,
Easter eggs and fancy fudge...

Go as far as you can with this poem until *x, y* and *z* cause real problems – then cheat! Try, for example, *x-ceptionally sticky toffee / yummy yellow sherbet dabs / zippy Zubes*. With the children's help, read this new ABC poem from the flip chart; encourage them to make it sound rhythmic.

Divide the children into five groups. Give each group a batch of letters (A–E, F–J, K–O, P–T, U–Z) and ask them to carry out a wordsearch, using the reference books to find a flower, bird or animal name, or a job that someone does, beginning with each of the letters allocated to them. You might need to help the group working with the letters U–Z, as all the most difficult words are in this section.

When they have done this, use their findings to scribe another alphabet poem on the flip chart. This time, look for matching 'doing words' (verbs), and encourage the children to make the poem as daft as they like. It works particularly well with 'jobs people do' – *actors abseiling* or *ambling*, *bakers bouncing* or *boxing*, and so on. The children will thoroughly enjoy this part of the activity! You might end up with:

Artists abseiling
Builders boxing
Cab drivers canoeing
Doctors dancing
Electricians eating
Firefighters foxtrotting... *and so on.*

The difficulty comes at the end again. Accept ingenious solutions such as *X-aminers x-raying, Youth leaders yodelling, Zoo-keepers zigzagging.*

Display the enlarged copy of the poem 'A–Z of beasts and eats' (photocopiable page 149) and read it aloud. Ask the children to think about the way that the poet has used the sequence of the alphabet in this poem. *Is it the same as the poems we have written together? If not, how is it different?*

Encourage the children to explore the form of this poem, noting the way in which the first word of each verse is a beast: *Alligators, Deer, Gorillas...* Use the alphabet chart to help the children work out the pattern. The first line

names a type of beast (*Alligators)*, the second line says what the beasts do (*bite*) and the third line says *what* they bite (*Coke cans*) – A, B, C. The next verse goes: *Deer* (beasts) / *eat* (what they do) / *fudge* (what they eat) – D, E, F. The poem follows the alphabet in three-letter sections. Once the children have established this pattern in their heads, read the poem aloud again for sheer enjoyment!

Finally, give out copies of photocopiable page 150. Let the children choose animals (perhaps minibeasts or birds) to fill in the right-hand spaces, then use describing words (adjectives) to complete the lines as before.

Suggestion(s) for extension
More confident children could follow the pattern of 'A-Z of beasts and eats' to create their own alphabet poems – for example, 'A-Z of people and party food':

Alice brings chocolate chips.
David enjoys fish fingers.
George hogs the ice-cream.
John knocks over the lemonade.
Michael nibbles oranges.
Poppy queues for raspberries.
Stewart tastes upside-down cake.
Vera wants xtra helpings.
Yasmin zips along to the party.

Suggestion(s) for support
Work through photocopiable page 150 with children who need support. Use a picture dictionary to help them to find words beginning with a particular letter. Encourage them to make up a humorous poem, so that they have *angry anteaters* or *aardvarks, beautiful buffalos* or *baboons* and so on, going for surreal ideas rather than logical ones. Ask the children to read their finished poems aloud to the rest of the class.

Assessment opportunities
Note those children who are familiar with the sequence of the alphabet, and can apply this knowledge to the use of reference books and dictionaries.

Opportunities for IT
Some children could use a word processor to write up their own alphabet poems. If the word processor has a thesaurus facility, they could use this to look for adjectives or verbs in order to complete the more difficult lines.

Display ideas
Construct a 26-page zigzag book or make a long wall-chart, inviting the children each to write and illustrate a page of the poem which you have scribed together. The zigzag book could be displayed standing up behind two tables with toys, pictures or other things that fit each of the five sections of the alphabet previously explored by the groups (see 'What to do').

Reference to photocopiable sheets
An enlarged (A3) copy or OHT of photocopiable page 149 should be displayed during the activity. Photocopiable page 150 is a writing frame for an animal alphabet poem; some children can work through it independently, and others can work through it with support from the teacher.

 ## KENNINGS

To recognize and write kennings, exploring their possibilities.

†† *Whole class, then pairs or small groups (including individual work).*

🕐 *40 minutes.*

Previous skills/knowledge needed
The children should be used to discussing ideas with others in the class and to listening with courtesy and attention. They should have a fairly wide vocabulary, and be accustomed to solving simple word puzzles.

Key background information
A **kenning** is a way of renaming something familiar using a compound word that tells you what the thing looks like or sounds like, but does not use its usual name. For example, snow might be described as a *grass-painter*, or the wind as a *door-rattler*. Kennings can be presented as word puzzles: the reader has to guess what thing has been renamed in this way. Exploring kennings is an excellent class exercise, and writing them helps to expand the children's vocabulary.

Preparation
It might be useful for you to work on a few starter ideas which capture the essential features of wind, snow, rain, thunder and so on, and can be developed into compound words. However, the children enjoy this activity so much that, once they know what it is all about, there is no stopping them!

Resources needed
A flip chart, writing materials.

What to do
Gather the children in the story area, preferably seated together on the carpet. Tell them that they must listen very carefully, because you have some word puzzles for them to solve. Talk about getting a birthday present through the post: how you shake the parcel, feel how heavy it is, look at the shape and so on to help you guess what is hidden inside.

Explain that this word puzzle is rather like a present in a

parcel: the name of the thing you are thinking about is hidden inside a different double word which gives them a clue. For example, ask the children what *a tree-shaker* might be. If they give an answer such as *A thing that shakes trees*, give a further clue by asking whether they can think of a kind of weather that could shake a tree. Once it is established that you are thinking of the wind, scribe *a tree-shaker* on the flip chart. Look at the way the double word is made up, with a hyphen joining the two words.

Scribe a few more examples of wind kennings on the flip chart. You might suggest *a wave-thrower, a gate-rattler, a dustbin-roller* and so on. Now ask the children to think about what a stormy wind does to slates on roofs: *knocks them off the roof, smashes them, cracks them...* Encourage the children to express these ideas in the form you have used – for example, *a slate-smasher, a slate-thrower, a slate-cracker*. Tell the children that these invented names are called **kennings**.

Suggest that the children try to invent more wind kennings. They could think first about the things that are affected by high winds: hats, branches, smoke, doors, windows and so on. Give the children a goal, say ten ideas, and scribe these in a list on the flip chart. The new wind kennings might include *a smoke-whirler, a branch-breaker, a hat-tosser, a door-slammer, a scarf-tangler* and so on.

Now that the children understand what kennings are and how they are constructed, suggest some more word puzzles for them to decipher. For example, ask them what is being described in each of the following groups of kennings:

▲ *A fire-drowner, a boat-floater, a body-washer, a tea-maker, a mud-mixer... What is it?* (Water.)

▲ *A night-lighter, a cloud-sailer, a shadow-maker, a space-dancer, a dark-chaser... What is it?* (The moon.)

▲ *A wellie-splasher, a puddle-maker, a hair-soaker, a flower-grower, a picnic-spoiler... What is it?* (Rain.)

Scribe these kennings on the flip chart so that the children can read them.

When they have worked out the answers to these, ask the children to try out a few of their own. Thunder makes a good subject for kennings. Encourage the children to think about the sound that thunder makes, where thunder comes from and when it arises. This will lead them to invent new descriptions that follow the kenning pattern, such as *a cloud-*

basher, a sky-drummer, a lightning-joiner, a storm-chaser, a cat-frightener and so on. Give the children a defined goal, say ten ideas for the class.

Once the kenning pattern is established and understood, the children will find it a highly enjoyable challenge. Divide the class into pairs or small groups of up to five children, and encourage the children in each group or pair to play against each other in thinking up kennings for other kinds of weather: snow, frost, fog, sunshine and so on. Suggest that they write perhaps six kennings for the topic they have chosen and then, after about five minutes, ask the others to solve their word puzzles: ... *What is it?*

Suggestion(s) for extension

Children who are independent writers could experiment with the form further. Ask them to think of an insect, an animal or a bird and then describe it using a kenning which says what the creature looks like, what it does or how it moves. For example, they might say that a cat likes to catch birds, enjoys sleeping in the sun, moves like a ballet dancer and so on. Let them write kennings which are describing rather than naming: *bird-catching, sun-seeking, butterfly-chasing* and so on.

Model a short poem based on these kennings on the flip chart. You need three double-word descriptions ending in *ing,* followed by an image (for example, a cat as a ballet dancer, a bird as a pop singer, a swallow as an acrobat, and so on). The poem might look like this:

Have you ever seen a cat?
a bird-catching
   sun-seeking
      butterfly-chasing
         ballet dancer?

or Have you ever seen a bird?
a worm-pulling
   nest-building
      sky-flying
         pop singer?

or Have you ever seen a swallow?
a high-flying
   space-swooping
      sky-diving
         trapeze artist?

Suggestion(s) for support

Children who need support could develop the wind kennings on the flip chart, perhaps suggesting a change in one word. For example, instead of *a tree-shaker,* they might suggest *a tree-bender, a tree-jiggler, a tree-swinger.* For *a wave-thrower,* they might try *a wave-crasher, a wave-ripper, a wave-pitcher* and so on. Or they might change the first word, *a wave-thrower* becoming *a hat-thrower, a hair-thrower, a tree-thrower* and so on. Using the suggestions already scribed on the flip chart will help to give these children confidence in their own verbal invention.

Assessment opportunities

Look for those children who enjoy playing with words, and who can suggest new descriptions that illuminate the characteristics of a subject. Note those who possess a suitably wide vocabulary. Watch out for those who need extra help to understand the pattern of a kenning.

Opportunities for IT

Some children could write their kennings using a word processor. They may need to be shown where the hyphen key is. They could experiment with different formats to increase their poem's impact.

The class set of kennings could be presented using a multimedia authoring package. Each kenning could be written and formatted on its own page, with a link to an answer page. Once readers have tried to guess what the answer is, they can click on the answer button and be shown whether they are right or wrong. Each kenning will need two pages of the presentation: one for the poem and the other for the answer. Figure 4 shows an example.

The presentation could be enhanced by adding the children's voices reciting their kennings, recorded with a microphone attached to the computer. Alternatively, single lines of each kenning could be presented one at a time, to let readers try to work out the answer before they see all of the clues. Once they think they have guessed it, they can click on the answer button to see.

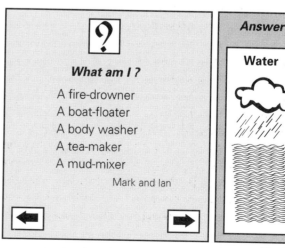

What am I ?

A fire-drowner
A boat-floater
A body washer
A tea-maker
A mud-mixer

Mark and Ian

Answer

Water

Figure 4

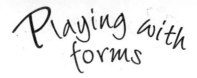

Figure 5

...gs can be written out on blue paper
...en on white paper, then cut out and glued
.... The children could hang the streamers
from a string across the hall, or attach them to plant sticks
and run outside with them.

The children can make books of kennings, as follows:
1. Fold an A4 sheet of thin card to make a tall double zigzag
(see Figure 5).
2. Write several kennings (for the same thing) going
downwards on the inside left-hand page, with the question
What is it? at the end.
3. Make a flap to conceal the answer on the right.
4. Write the title (for example, *Kennings of the weather*)
and the poet's name on the front page.

RECIPE FOR A SANDCASTLE

To write a poem using the format of a recipe.
✝✝ *Whole class, then individual work.*
🕐 *45 minutes.*

Previous skills/knowledge needed
The children should be able to share ideas with one another.
They should know what a recipe is, and that people often
use recipes for cooking. They should be aware of how
instructions can form a sequence (for example, in baking a
cake). They should also be familiar with a few simple baking
terms: *take, add, mix, stir, decorate with* and so on.

Key background information
This activity involves writing poems based loosely on the
recipe format. It is an ideal follow-up to a baking session
with volunteer helpers. The idea of a 'recipe poem' is used
in a more metaphorical way in *Curriculum Bank Poetry (Key
Stage 2)*; here it is used more literally, with a view to
developing the children's awareness of sequence.

Preparation
Collect a number of illustrated recipe books. Make one copy
per child of photocopiable page 151. If you have a sand
tray in the classroom, keep it to hand. It would be useful,
but it is not essential, to provide some seashells.

Resources needed
Illustrated recipe books, photocopiable page 151, a sand
tray, water, seashells (optional), a flip chart, writing
materials.

What to do
Group the children in a comfortable area, making sure that
everyone can see the flip chart and the recipe books.
Introduce the activity by talking with the children about
cooking meals and baking cakes. *Who does the cooking in
school? Which school meals do you like best/least? Does
anyone help with baking cakes or making dinner at home?*
If some children have helped with cooking, discuss what
they did: collecting things that were needed, opening
packets, mixing food, washing up and so on. *Have you
watched a meal being prepared? How is a ready-made meal
cooked?* Some children may have seen food being heated
up in a microwave or conventional oven.

*If your parent or grandparent wanted to bake a cake,
what kind of book would they use?* (A recipe book.) *What
do recipe books tell you?* The children might say: 'They tell
you the things you need. They tell you what to do. They
show you pictures of what the cakes will look like.' Show
the children some of the illustrated recipe books, letting
some point out cakes or sweets that they would like to
eat. Ask whether they know the things needed to bake a
cake; list *flour, sugar, eggs, milk, currants* and so on on the
flip chart. Tell them, or elicit the fact, that 'the things you
need' are called **ingredients**.

Tell the children that together, you are going to write a
recipe poem called 'Recipe for a sandcastle', following the
pattern set by the cookery books. If you have access to a
sand tray, ask two children to demonstrate how they go
about making a sandcastle. Then say that the poem is going
to be about building a castle on the beach, not in the sand
tray – so you will need to gather all the ingredients first.
Ask them to think about everything they need to make a
sandcastle: *the seashore, sand, water, a spade, shells* and
so on.

On the flip chart, scribe *Recipe for a sandcastle*;
underneath, write the word *Take*. Tell the children that this
is a simple way of saying 'what you need'. Ask them when
and where they would be likely to build a sandcastle, and
scribe their response: *Take a hot day* or *a trip to the seaside*
or *a day by the sea*. Alternatively, listing things that you
simply need to have: *sand, water, a spade...*

Show the children how you might arrange some of these ideas into lines – for example:

Take a hot day   or   Take some sand,
by the seaside   a red spade
with sparkling waves.   and a bucket of water.

Following the recipe format, use the word Add to say what else you need:

Add a red spade,   or   Add some sunshine,
some golden sand   one white cloud
and water from the sea.   and the sound of the
                               sea.

Demonstrate how the poem can use more recipe words such as stir, mix, decorate with, top with and so on:

Mix well, pat   or   Stir sand and water,
smooth and   let it dry in the sun
decorate with shells.   and top with a flag.

And you have made   And you have made
   a sandcastle!   a sandcastle!

Look at the two poems scribed side by side. *What things are the same? What things are different?* The children might suggest:

▲ Both poems start with *Take* and end with *And you have made a sandcastle!*
▲ They both use the word *Add*.
▲ One poem uses *Mix*, the other uses *Stir*.
▲ Both poems have three lines in each verse.
.... and so on.

Working orally, let the children see how they could use this format to make up a 'Recipe for a snowman'. They should think first about what they will need: *a cold winter's day, lots of snow, a spade, a scarf, a hat, a carrot for the nose...* Remind them that they should start with the word *Take*. Thus they might suggest:

Take a cold winter's day, or Take some deep white snow
bare black trees   a heavy spade
and the sun as red as fire.   and lots of hard work.

They should go on to think about what they might add – for example:

   Add a long woollen scarf
   a black hat
   and a carrot for his nose.

   And you have made
      a snowman!

Give out copies of photocopiable page 151. Show the children that this writing frame is set out in recipe form, all ready for their snowman poems. If they need help with spelling, scribe some of the words they will use on the flip chart. Let them complete the poems in their own way.

When they have finished, ask some of the children to

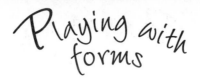

read their work aloud. Offer comments and congratulations, especially where a child has used a new and surprising idea.

Suggestion(s) for extension
Let those children who are independent writers discuss how they might adapt the format to make other recipe poems – for example, a recipe for a kite or a tent. They might produce poems such as the following:

Recipe for a kite	**Recipe for a tent**
Take some red paper, two criss-cross sticks and a long string with bows.	Take an old sheet a long pole and two chairs back to back.
Add a sunny day a tall grassy hill and a cool blue breeze.	Add a garden lawn, a picnic and two noisy little boys.
And you have made a kite! Go fly it!	And you have made a tent! Go hide away!

Suggestion(s) for support
Children who need support with writing could discuss with an adult helper the things they would need to build a snowman. He or she should scribe a list from their suggestions. The children can then simply choose from the list to fill the spaces on photocopiable page 151.

Assessment opportunities
Look for those children who suggest unusual ideas for their poems, especially in the backgrounds they choose (for example, *and the whisper of the waves* or *and a cool, blue breeze*). Look for those who work independently on their lines until they have a satisfactory rhythm.

Opportunities for IT
The children could use a word processor to write their poems. If they initially write a complete sentence on each line, they can be shown how to break the lines up using the Return key or join them together using the Delete key. They may need some practice with this before they understand how it works. (Some very simple word processors do not have a Delete key, so check before you start.)

The children could also use an art package to create a picture of their sandcastle or snowman and add it to their poem. Alternatively, the poem could be written onto a picture of a seaside or snowy scene. To do this, the children will need to know how to place text on the screen within the art package, changing the font size and style to make it fit in the space available. They might even break up the poem into several short sections to fit around the picture.

Display ideas
Working together, the children can paint a large seaside scene and a large snow scene, displaying them side by side so that the contrasting colours and different kinds of weather are evident. They can show a huge sandcastle in one picture and a snowman in the other. They can each paint an appropriately dressed child on a smaller sheet of paper and cut it out. The pictures of children should be grouped, collage-style, around the centre-piece of each scene. The children's recipe poems can be placed around the collages, with a collection of recipe books and artefacts (bobble hats and woollen gloves for the snow scene; buckets, spades and sun-glasses for the beach scene) placed on tables underneath.

Reference to photocopiable sheet
Photocopiable page 151 is a writing frame which should be given to the children for independent work, as a follow-up to the shared writing in the activity.

Recipe poem writing frame

Recipe for a snowman

Take _____

and _____

Add _____

and _____

Stir in _____

and _____

Decorate with _____

and _____

And you have made a snowman!

SHAPE POEMS

To explore, discuss and write shape poems, paying particular attention to word-choice and visual presentation. To select concrete poems for a class anthology.

†† *Whole class, then individual and paired work.*

🕐 *40 minutes.*

Previous skills/knowledge needed

The children should have a reasonably wide vocabulary at their command. They should be able to relate their language skills to the challenge of presenting words on the page. They need to be confident about sharing their ideas orally with other members of the class.

Key background knowledge

A **shape poem** uses language arranged into the shape of the subject of the poem. There are two main types of shape poem:

▲ In a **calligram**, the letters of the words are enlarged or distorted to suggest the subject of the poem.

▲ In a **concrete poem**, the physical arrangement of the words on the page suggests the subject of the poem.

This activity is concerned mostly with concrete poems ('Climb the mountain' on page 152 is both a calligram and a concrete poem). It explores and develops the children's range of language, and should make use of 'word-trading' (see page 10) – that is, not accepting the first word or idea offered, but building up and extending a list of vocabulary from the children's suggestions. Encourage the children to choose the best or most unusual words they can find. The shapes of the concrete poems should be kept simple, using outlines only.

Preparation

Make enlarged (A3) copies or OHTs of the poems on photocopiable pages 152, 153 and 154 for display. Make one copy per child of photocopiable page 155, and some copies of photocopiable page 156 (see 'Suggestion(s) for support'). Find some anthologies and collections of poetry which include shape poems, such as *Madtail, Miniwhale and Other Shape Poems* edited by Wes Magee (Puffin, 1991).

Resources needed

Photocopiable pages 152 to 156, anthologies and collections of poetry, a flip chart, writing materials, felt-tipped pens or coloured pencils.

What to do

Gather the children together in the story corner and make sure that everyone will have a clear view of the flip chart and the enlarged poems.

Discuss with the children what they think a poem is, and what poems look like. Depending on their previous experience, the children may make comments such as: *poems are in lines; some poems rhyme; poems have verses; poems describe things; some poems tell a story;* and so on.

Tell the children that they are going to look at a new kind of poem: one that uses its words to make a kind of picture. Without giving the children time to read the poem, quickly show them the enlarged copy of 'Climb the mountain' (photocopiable page 152). Ask them to guess from its shape what the poem is about. They may suggest *a hill, a roof, a tent...* Now put the poem up where it can be seen easily and read it aloud. Point out the words as you go along, so that the children can see that the words themselves make a mountain shape. Show them that you have to read this poem in a different way from usual: starting at the bottom and reading up, then reading down again from the top.

'Climb the mountain' is not written in verse form, but it does have a rhyme pattern. Ask the children to find the rhyming words: *high/sky, blow/below*. Now ask the children to read the poem with you, looking for the senses words that the poet has used: *touch the clouds, see the sky, feel the wind...* Ask the children to suggest other senses words that the poet might have used – for example, *listen to the wind, taste the cold air...*

Ask whether there are any other features of the way the poem is written that makes it different from those they are used to: *the size of the letters, big at first, then they go small...* Discuss why this might be so and what the poet is telling us: *that it's a hard climb, you get tired at the top, and it's a long way down!*

Now work on 'shower' (photocopiable page 153) in a similar way. Let the children glance quickly at the shape of the poem and then guess what it is about. They may suggest *stairs, slates on the roof, step-ladders...* Encourage them to explore these ideas further; for example, it might be *a not wanting to go to bed poem, a Father Christmas on the roof poem, a putting up wallpaper poem...*

Tell the children that the poem is called 'shower'. Display the enlarged copy where it can be seen clearly and read it aloud. Again, point out how the words are read: not in the conventional way, but going downwards in diagonal strips.

101

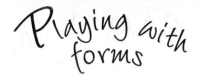

Ask the children how many verses there are in 'shower'. *What makes these four verses look different from the normal ones? Does the poem rhyme?* Ask the children to look for rhymes in the poem: *rain/drain, street/feet, sky/high, out/shout* and so on.

Encourage the children to explore the poem with their eyes, looking at how the poet has written each description of something in the poem. The descriptions are written in sets of three words – for example, *cars make spray / birds huddle away / cats lie asleep / plants drink deep*. Have the children noticed that there are no capital letters or full stops in this poem? Discuss why this might be. Read the poem aloud together, encouraging the children to picture the scene in their minds.

Display the enlarged copy of 'Snow-stroll' (photocopiable page 154). This is a quite different kind of shape poem. *What picture are the words intended to make?* (Footsteps in the snow.) Read the poem aloud to the children, letting them follow the words as you do so. Explore the way that the poet has used exciting language to describe the marks left in the snow and the sounds his feet make: *the crispy patterns... the crunchy sound*. Can the children think of other words that he might have used? They may suggest *the starry shapes, the shivery sound, the crackly sound...*

The author says that he changes direction in the snow. Ask a child to show with his or her fingers how the poet has used the pattern of words on the page to show himself *changing direction*. Read out the poem again, with the children joining in.

The last two poems have been about the weather. Ask the children to collect sun words that could be used to make a sun-shape poem. They should try to think of words which describe how the sun looks (*bright, fiery, sparkling, shining, golden*), its shape (*round, like a wheel, like a pound coin*) and how it feels (*burning, hot, fierce, scorching*). Scribe the children's words and phrases on the flip chart.

Now give out copies of photocopiable page 155. The children will see that the sun's rays are outlined on the sheet. Ask them to make a sun-shape poem by choosing words and ideas from the flip chart and writing them along the lines of the rays. When they have finished, they can illustrate their work with coloured pencils or felt-tipped pens. Then they can display their shape poems and read them aloud.

Conclude the activity by asking the children to work in pairs, looking through poetry anthologies and collections to find more examples of shape poems to show to the class. Encourage them to explain how they think these poems have been put together and how they should be read aloud – for example, going upward from the roots to the topmost branch in a tree poem; going round and round, spiralwise, in a football poem; and so on. They could put the shape poems they have found together in a 'Big Book' class anthology.

Suggestion(s) for extension

A group of independent writers could look closely at the way in which 'Snow-stroll' has been put together, then write a 'copycat' poem about walking on the sand. Ask them to think about the heat of a summer's day, the marks that their bare feet would make on the sand, the feel and sound of sand under their feet, and so on. They might start their 'Sand-stroll' poem in a similar way to the John Walsh poem – for example:

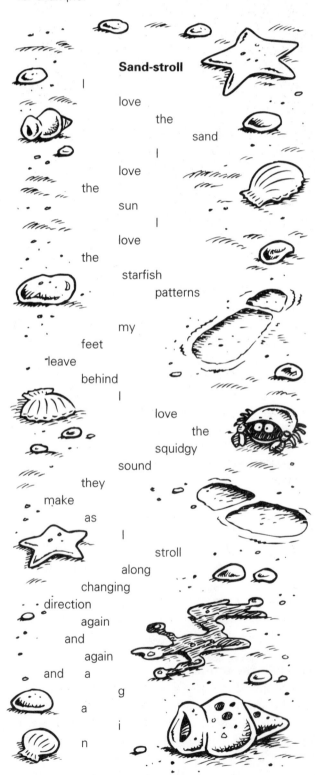

Sand-stroll

I
love
the
sand
I
love
the
sun
I
love
the
starfish
patterns
my
feet
leave
behind
I
love
the
squidgy
sound
they
make
as
I
stroll
along
changing
direction
again
and
again
and a
g
a
i
n

horizontally, as in 'Climb the mountain'. It would be difficult to write the 'sunshine' shape poem (for example) using a traditional word processor, since the words would need to be printed at different angles. However, some more recent word processors (such as Textease) and simple desktop publishing programs allow children to rotate text, so that they can print lines at different angles.

An alternative method which is more flexible is to use a drawing package. In this software, each word or phrase becomes a separate 'object' that can be moved anywhere on the page, turned and rotated to any position and sometimes even bent into a curved shape. Young children may need help with this software if it is new to them.

Display ideas

Shape poems are a display in themselves! Encourage the children to exploit the possibilities by presenting their written work with care. They can use red and orange pencil crayons or fine felt-tipped pens for their sun poems, either working on photocopiable page 155 or transferring their finished work to yellow paper; the sun poem can be cut out as a circle and backed with sky-blue paper. Ask the children to draw and cut out some children dressed for the sun; these figures can make a colourful border for the poems.

The children might enjoy trying another poem of this kind, this time about walking along a twisty road in the rain. They should be encouraged to write out their poems in 'best', so that they not only sound good but look good as well!

Suggestion(s) for support

Children who need support can work in pairs with more able children, choosing 'rain' words to fill in a simple pattern on a copy of photocopiable page 156. Encourage the more confident partners to explain how they might choose words to describe how the rain looks, sounds and feels – for example:

wet	*stormy*	*grey*
dripping	thunder	plopping
dropping	lightning	puddles
soaking	cloudy	pouring

Assessment opportunities

Look for those children who find it easy to combine the idea of shape with the use of interesting language.

Opportunities for IT

Some shape poems can be written and formatted using a word processor. This is one time when children will need to position the words on the screen using the Space bar. Before you start this work, it is important to know what your word processor can and can't do with text. The easiest poems to format are those where the words are written

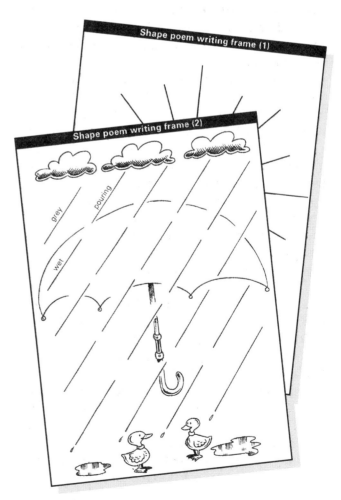

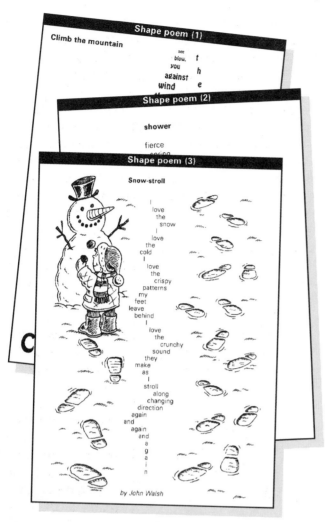

Reference to photocopiable sheets

The poems on photocopiable pages 152, 153 and 154 should be enlarged to A3 size or copied onto OHTs for display during the lesson. Photocopiable page 155 is a pictorial writing frame: the children can fill in 'sun words' along the sun's rays to make a simple but effective shape poem. Photocopiable page 156 is an additional pictorial writing frame which less able children can use for consolidation, working with a partner to write 'rain words' along the slanted lines.

RIDDLES

To appreciate riddles as a form of poetry and to write their own riddles.

†† *Whole class, then pairs.*

🕐 *40 minutes (a follow-up session may be needed).*

Previous skills/knowledge needed

The children should be able to observe everyday objects closely, and to write about them in simple descriptive language. It would be helpful, but is not essential, for them to have some experience of using simile and metaphor.

Key background knowledge

Riddling is a very old form of poetry, with a long tradition behind it. Children enjoy the puzzle aspect of riddle poems, and can appreciate their playful use of images. Encourage the children to use language clues in constructing their own riddles and in solving ones written by other children. This activity is a good introduction to writing in the first person, taking an 'imaginative leap' into the viewpoint of an object or an animal.

Preparation

Make an enlarged (A3) copy or OHT of photocopiable page 157. Make a collection of small familiar objects (for example, a sharp pencil, an egg, an ice lolly, a marble and so on). Include a few models or pictures of minibeasts (ladybirds, spiders, butterflies, bees and so on). Find a picture or photograph of a hen.

Resources needed

Photocopiable page 157, a collection of objects or pictures (as above), a photograph or picture of a hen, a flip chart, blank paper, writing materials.

What to do

Gather the children in the story corner. Make sure that everyone will have a good view of the flip chart, objects and pictures.

Tell the children that you are going to read a special kind of poem called a **riddle**. Explain that a riddle is a word-puzzle. They have to listen carefully and guess what the poet is writing about. Read 'Riddle' (from photocopiable page 157) aloud, saying only that it describes something that lives in the farmyard. What clues does the poet give? *It's a fat brown bird.* What about the legs? *Thin pink legs.* So what is it? *It's a hen!*

Show the children the enlarged version of 'Riddle'. Explore with them some of the language the poet has used: *speckled, feather-fluffed...* What do these descriptions tell us about the hen? *It's fat with feathers, all fluffy, a bit spotty...* What does the poet mean by *and a red party hat*? It doesn't really mean the hen is going to a party! Show the children the picture of a hen. Ask them about the comb on top of the hen's head: what shape is it? *It's got spiky bits like a Queen's crown. It looks like she's wearing a red hat...* And the spiky bits make it look like? *A party hat!*

Explain that in writing a riddle, poets often take on the viewpoint of the riddle's subject. They may ask the question *What am I?* at the end. The riddle describes something as if it were alive and compares it to something else, so that the reader has to work out a puzzle to find out what the subject is.

Look again at the picture of the hen. What might the poet have said about the hen's eyes? *They are little, shiny and round.* What do they look like? *Like shiny black beads,*

like tiny bright buttons... What does the hen's body look like? *Like a feather duster on legs, like an empty bird's nest...* Encourage the children to appreciate the potential for use of images in the writing of a riddle.

Read the poem aloud together, with one group saying the verse, another asking the final question and all together answering: *I'm a hen!*

Now read 'Riddle of the pond' aloud. The title of this poem gives the reader a clue: where does this thing live? *In a pond.* Ask the children to search the poem for more clues – for example, *it is shiny, it twists and turns, sometimes you see it and sometimes you don't...* Can you guess what it is? *A fish.* Yes – what kind of fish? *Is it a goldfish?* What words make you think it's a goldfish? *'I shine like a jewel...'*

Ask the children why they think the poet says *I flash... like an underwater firework.* Suggest that they think about the movement of a fish. What words might describe it? *Zipping, sizzling, whirling, flashing...* just like fireworks! What might *the deep sunken forest* be? *Waterlilies, water weeds, the roots of plants...* What does the line *Now you see me, now you don't'?* describe? *Goldfish sometimes come to the top of the pond then dive back deep down, very quickly.* Ask the children for images to describe what the goldfish are like – for example, *like fireworks, like bubbles, like fallen stars, like jewels...*

Read the riddle aloud with the children, changing the groups around from the last time: one group reading the verse, another asking the final question, then all together answering *I'm a goldfish!*

Now read 'Riddle of summer' aloud. Ask the children to work as before, looking for clues. What can they tell about this thing? *It lives in the air. It used to live in a pond. It moves very fast. It is **iridescent**.* What does that mean? *Coloured like a rainbow, shiny like tinfoil...* What is it? *A dragonfly.*

Encourage the children to look at the language the poet has used to give these clues – for example, *a small iridescent twig, / Silver wrapped like a thin sweet.* Ask them to paint the dragonfly's picture in their heads. Have any of the children seen a dragonfly? If so, how else do they think

the poet could have described this creature? *Like a transparent helicopter, like a Twiglet with rainbow wings...* The poet says the dragonfly is *a catch-sun.* Discuss what this might mean. Look at the ending: *You look again: I've gone!* Dragonflies don't hang about for long!

Follow the same procedure as before: ask the class to read the poem aloud, then ask and answer the question.

Now tell the children that together, you will write a riddle about an object or picture which you have produced from your collection – for example, the egg. Remind them that they must not give the answer away, so the word 'egg' must not be used. They should try to think about what it looks like: *like a tennis ball, like a stone, like a round box...* What does the shell feel like? *Smooth as ice, breakable as glass...* Scribe some of the children's images on the flip chart.

Remind the children that they must make it sound as though the riddle were made up by the egg itself! Encourage them to find an opening line, such as *I am a box* or *I am a thin-skinned stone* or *I am like a freckled face.* The riddle might begin to look like this:

Figure 6

Riddle of the supermarket
I'm like a freckled stone,
as smooth as glass,
a box without a lock,
cream and brown outside,
yellow and white inside.
Take care! Don't drop me!
What am I?

Ask the children to work in pairs, choosing another object or picture from your collection and hiding it in the words of a riddle. Give out blank paper and writing materials. Suggest that they first make a list of things that their chosen subject looks like, thinking about its colour and shape; then what it feels like; and so on. They should then rearrange their suggestions, one idea to a line, describing the object as though it were describing itself. The first line should begin with *I am...* or *I am like...* The riddle should finish with the question *What am I?*

Give the children 5–10 minutes to draft their riddles. When they have finished, let them try their riddles out on the rest of the class. (Save this for a follow-up session if necessary.)

Suggestion(s) for extension

Ask those children who are confident independent writers to work on a riddle describing the weather. As before, they should start by gathering ideas about what the weather looks and feels like. Then they should put together an image poem – for example:

Riddle of the sky

I am like a skipping rope
twisting high in the air.
I am like paint
splashed across the sky.
Sometimes I feel rain.
Sometimes I feel sunshine.
I have secret treasure.
What am I?

Suggestion(s) for support

Work with a group of children who are not yet confident writers. Take a familiar classroom object, such as a pencil, and help the children to look at it in new ways (following the procedure already modelled on the flip chart).

Stand the pencil on its end and ask what it looks like. *A tower, a lighthouse, a factory chimney...* Let the children choose the idea they like best and scribe, for example, *I look like a tower.*

Let the children feel how sharp the pencil is: *sharp as a sword, sharp as a pin...* What is it made of? *Wood and lead.* What is it used for? *To help you write, to put words on paper...* Scribe their ideas into a simple riddle form. It might look like this:

A classroom riddle

I look like a tower.
I am as sharp as a pin.
I have a wooden skin
and a body made of lead.
I help you write poems.
What am I?

Let the children try to baffle the class with their riddle.

Assessment opportunities

Look for those children:

▲ who can use and understand image (in the form of simile or metaphor);

▲ whose vocabulary is extensive;

▲ who can 'see' the answer to a riddle.

Opportunities for IT

Some children could draft their riddles using a word processor. They may need to be shown how to rearrange the lines using the 'cut and paste' or 'drag and drop' techniques. A framework file could be created in advance to help the children get started more quickly.

The completed riddles could all be word-processed and made into a class anthology (perhaps in 'big book' format) of riddles. The answers could appear on a separate page at the end of the book. The pages could be illustrated with pictures created with an art package or scanned from the children's drawings. A more ambitious project would be to create a multimedia presentation using authoring software, as in 'Kennings' (see page 97).

Display ideas

Let the children make puzzle books. Give them a square of paper or thin card, folded as shown in Figure 6. They can write the name of the poem on the outside cover, the riddle on the inside left-hand page and the answer behind a flap on the inside right-hand page. They can decorate their riddle cards using felt-tipped pens – remembering not to draw the answer!

Reference to photocopiable sheet

Photocopiable page 157 features three riddles which can be read out and discussed by the children and used as models for their own writing. The answers are: a dragonfly, a goldfish, a hen. The sheet should be enlarged to A3 size or copied onto an OHT for whole-class use.

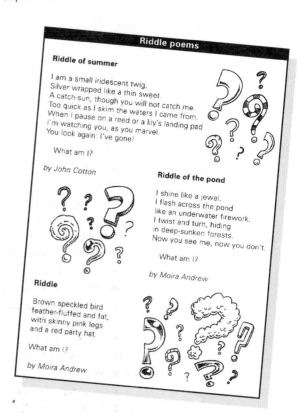

Riddle poems

Riddle of summer

I am a small iridescent twig,
Silver wrapped like a thin sweet.
A catch-sun, though you will not catch me.
Too quick as I skim the waters I came from.
When I pause on a reed or a lily's landing pad
I'm watching you, as you marvel.
You look again: I've gone!

What am I?

by John Cotton

Riddle of the pond

I shine like a jewel.
I flash across the pond
like an underwater firework.
I twist and turn, hiding
in deep-sunken forests.
Now you see me, now you don't.

What am I?

by Moira Andrew

Riddle

Brown speckled bird
feather-fluffed and fat,
with skinny pink legs
and a red party hat.

What am I?

by Moira Andrew

Photocopiables

The pages in this section can be photocopied for use in the classroom or school which has purchased this book, and do not need to be declared in any return in respect of any photocopying licence.

They comprise a varied selection of both pupil and teacher resources, including pupil worksheets, resource material and record sheets to be completed by the teacher or children. Most of the photocopiable pages are related to individual activities in the book; the name of the activity is indicated at the top of the sheet, together with a page reference indicating where the lesson plan for that activity can be found.

Individual pages are discussed in detail within each lesson plan, accompanied by ideas for adaptation where appropriate – of course, each sheet can be adapted to suit your own needs and those of your class. Sheets can also be coloured, laminated, mounted on to card, enlarged and so on where appropriate.

Pupil worksheets and record sheets have spaces provided for children's names and for noting the date on which each sheet was used. This means that, if so required, they can be included easily within any pupil assessment portfolio.

Weather sounds, see page 18

A poem of sounds

Weather is full of the Nicest Sounds

Weather is full
of the nicest sounds:
it sings
and rustles
and pings
and pounds
and hums
and tinkles
and strums
and twangs
and whishes
and sprinkles
and splishes
and bangs
and mumbles
and grumbles
and rumbles
and flashes
and crashes.

I wonder
if thunder
frightens a bee,
a mouse in her house,
a bird in a tree?
A bear
or a hare
or a fish in the sea?

Not me!

by Aileen Fisher

Kate's skates, see page 20

A rhyming poem

Easy peasy!

'Easy peasy! easy peasy!' said Kate –
''Course I can skate, 'course I can skate,
You should see me – just wait
Till you see my super figure-of-eight,
And my spins and jumps, they're just great.'

Out on the skating rink went Kate,
Sure and steady and ever so straight.
'Easy peasy! easy peasy!' yelled Kate –
'Now watch, I'll do my figure-of-eight.
Here I go now – just you wait.'

Then ... Whoops! Down in the icy slush went Kate,
Splatter splat! – flat as a plate.
Mum said, 'Look at you! Look at you Kate!
However did you get in such a state?'

'Oh! easy peasy! easy peasy!' grinned Kate.

by David Whitehead

POETRY

Kate's skates, see page 20

Pictures for rhymes

Writing frame

One, two, _____

Three, four, _____

Five, six, _____

Seven, eight, _____

Nine, ten, _____

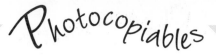

Food, glorious food! see page 26

Food poems (1)

The Cupboard

I know a little cupboard,
With a teeny tiny key,
And there's a jar of Lollipops
   For me, me, me.

It has a little shelf, my dear,
As dark as dark can be,
And there's a dish of Banbury Cakes
   For me, me, me.

I have a small fat grandmamma,
With a very slippery knee,
And she's Keeper of the Cupboard,
   With the key, key, key.

And when I'm very good, my dear,
As good as good can be,
There's Banbury Cakes, and Lollipops
   For me, me, me.

by Walter de la Mare

The hardest thing in the world to do

The hardest thing in the world to do
is to stand in the hot sun
at the end of a long queue for ice-creams
watching all the people who've just bought theirs
coming away from the queue
giving their ice-creams their very first lick.

by Michael Rosen

Food, glorious food! see page 26

Food poems (2)

Picnic-packaged

I peel my bendy banana,
unzipping its thick yellow coat
and think of how far it has journeyed
across the seas on a boat.

Once it grew like a finger
on a giant's bunched-up hand,
high on a tree in the sunshine
in the fields of a faraway land.

I bite into the creamy-white flesh
of my picnic-packaged food –
after coming half-way round the world
I'm surprised it tastes so good!

by Moira Andrew

Harvest Festival

Cabbages, cauliflowers,
   crisp, crunchy swedes,
   peppers and parsnips
   and melons with seeds;
Onions and mushrooms,
   potatoes for chips,
   tomatoes, bananas
   and apples with pips;
Stick beans and broad beans
   and beans in a tin,
   blackcurrants so juicy
   they run down your chin;
Cornflakes for breakfast
   and mangoes for tea –
Come to our harvest
   and give thanks with me.

by Irene Yates

Food, glorious food! see page 26

Food poems (3)

Cake for tea

Mix a cake,
   whisk a cake,
pop it in the tin!

Bake a cake,
   cool a cake,
please may I begin?

Cut a cake,
   slice a cake,
put it on the plate.

Pass a cake,
   share a cake,
do I have to wait?

Bite a cake,
   chew a cake,
eat up every crumb.

Empty plate,
   no more cake,
all down in my tum!

by Moira Andrew

Breakfast for One

Hot thick crusty buttery toast
Buttery toasty thick hot crust
Crusty buttery hot thick toast
Crusty thick hot toasty butter
Thick hot buttery crusty toast
Toasty buttery hot thick crust
Hot buttery thick crusty toast –

with marmalade is how I like it
most!

by Judith Nicholls

Breakfast boast, see page 29

Dragon poem (1)

Breakfast boast

The smoke alarm went off one day –
our dad expected the worst.
He dialled 999 in his head;
he prayed and yelled and cursed.

Downstairs, no flames, no heroics,
just a wisp of pearly smoke
and a tiny scaly creature. 'What's
this?' said dad. 'Some kind of joke?'

The little dragon looked so sad,
crying floods of great fat tears
that dad forgot to be angry. He
tickled its forest-green ears.

Eyes shining like sparks, ash on
its face, the creature started to puff.
'I'm lost,' it wept and out shot a flame –
'Hey,' growled dad. 'That's quite enough!'

'We'll put you to work, my lad,' said
dad and now it's our proudest boast,
we're the only family in our street
with a *DRAGON* to make breakfast toast!

by Moira Andrew

Breakfast boast, see page 29

Dragon lines

The smoke alarm went off one day –

our dad expected the worst.

He dialled 999 in his head;

he prayed and yelled and cursed.

Downstairs, no flames, no heroics,

just a wisp of pearly smoke

and a tiny scaly creature. 'What's

this?' said dad. 'Some kind of joke?'

The little dragon looked so sad,

crying floods of great fat tears

that dad forgot to be angry. He

tickled its forest-green ears.

Eyes shining like sparks, ash on

its face, the creature started to puff.

'I'm lost,' it wept and out shot a flame –

'Hey,' growled dad. 'That's quite enough!'

'We'll put you to work, my lad,' said

dad and now it's our proudest boast,

we're the only family in our street

with a *DRAGON* to make breakfast toast!

by Moira Andrew

A small dragon, see page 32

Dragon poem (2)

A Small Dragon

I've found a small dragon in the woodshed.
Think it must have come from deep inside a forest
because it's damp and green and leaves
are still reflecting in its eyes.

I fed it on many things, tried grass,
the roots of stars, hazel-nut and dandelion,
but it stared up at me as if to say, I need
food you can't provide.

It made a nest among the coal,
not unlike a bird's but larger,
it is out of place here
and is quite silent.

If you believed in it I would come
hurrying to your house to let you share my wonder,
but I want instead to see
if you yourself will pass this way.

by Brian Patten

A small dragon, see page 32

A dragon picture

The secret brother, see page 35

A mystery poem

The Secret Brother

Jack lived in the green-house
When I was six,
With glass and with tomato plants,
Not with slates and bricks.

I didn't have a brother,
Jack became mine.
Nobody could see him,
He never gave a sign.

Just beyond the rockery,
By the apple-tree,
Jack and his old mother lived,
Only for me.

With a tin telephone
Held beneath the sheet,
I would talk to Jack each night.
We would never meet.

Once my sister caught me,
Said, "He isn't there.
Down among the flower-pots
Cramm the gardener

Is the only person."
I said nothing, but
Let her go on talking.
Yet I moved Jack out.

He and his old mother
Did a midnight flit.
No one knew his number:
I had altered it.

Only I could see
The sagging washing-line
And my brother making
Our own secret sign.

by Elizabeth Jennings

What nonsense! see page 37

Nonsense poems (1)

Peter Piper picked a peck of pickled pepper,
   A peck of pickled pepper Peter Piper picked.
If Peter Piper picked a peck of pickled pepper,
   Where's the peck of pickled pepper Peter Piper picked?

Anonymous

Say Please

I'll have a please sandwich cheese
No I mean a knees sandwich please
Sorry I mean a fleas sandwich please
No a please sandwich please
no   no –
I'll have a doughnut

by Michael Rosen

Wild Flowers

The thought of a fox
Ever putting on socks,
Is silly, my love,
Yet here's a foxglove.

Pray, tell me what flower
Can tell you the hour
Without a tick-tock?
A dandelion clock.

I read in a rhyme
Of flowers that chime;
This didn't ring true,
Yet bluebells seem to.

part of a poem by Colin West

What nonsense! see page 37

Nonsense poems (2)

Says of the Week

Money-day. Pay away day.
Choose day. Whose day?
Wedding's day. Thick or thin day.
Furs day. Wrap up warm day.
Fries day. Hot dog day.
Sat-a-day. Armchair day.
Sons day. Dads play.

by John Foster

Eataweek

Bunsday
Stewsday
Henseggday
Burgerday
Pieday
Spaghettiday
Sundae.

by John Coldwell

Poems by Judith Nicholls (1)

When?

Where will you take me, magic horse,
with your mane-like wings unfurled?
Will you take me high through the
                    midnight sky?

We'll see the world!

How will you take me, magic horse,
do you ride on a magic track?
Your shoes are gold, so I've been told . . .

They'll bring us back!

When will you take me, magic horse,
with the clover on your brow?
When shall we race through starry space?

I'll take you now!

by Judith Nicholls

Magic

A web
captures the storm:
glass beads, safe in fine net,
gather sunlight as they sway in
high winds.

by Judith Nicholls

Poems by Judith Nicholls (2)

Sack race

Toes in,
knees in.
Quick now,
squeeze in!
Itchy back,
tickle-knees,
hairy sack
makes you sneeze.
Two-feet-hop,
never stop!
Snap, snip,
don't trip . . .
There and back
jumping sack . . .
One . . .
    two . . .
        three . . .
           OFF!

by Judith Nicholls

Timeless

There is no clock in the forest
but a dandelion to blow,
an owl that hunts
when the light has gone,
a mouse that sleeps
till night has come,
lost in the moss below.

There is no clock in the forest,
only the cuckoo's song
and the thin white
of the early dawn,
the pale damp-bright
of a waking June,
the bluebell light
of a day half-born
when the stars have gone.

There is no clock in the forest.

by Judith Nicholls

Sounds like this, see page 44

Sound poems (1)

Metal Fettle

The clank of a tank
the chink of chains
the tinkle of tins
the rattle of trains.

The click of a clasp
the clang of a bell
the creak of a hinge
the chime of a spell.

The shatter of cymbals
the clash of swords
the clatter of cutlery
the twang of chords.

The ping of keys
the song of a wheel
the plink of pans
the ring of steel.

by John Rice

Kitchen sounds

Porridge gloops
A sausage sizzles
The toaster clangs
The kettle whistles
Washing spins
People chatter
Knives chop
Dishes clatter
Taps gush
Pans clink
Water gurgles
In the sink.

The light clicks off
Night-time comes
And in the dark
The freezer hums.

by Richard James

Sound poems (2)

Storm trouble

The rain
          pops
                    drops,
Out of spongy clouds.
As,
the wind
          whirls,
                    swirls,
Round bony fingered trees.
And
the lightning
          clashes
                    flashes,
Across a frightened face of sky.
While,
the storm
          thunders
                    blunders,
In its search for somewhere to hang,
Its dark cloak of weathery trouble.

by Ian Souter

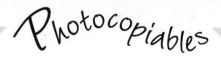

The secret creature, see page 48

Writing frame

The secret creature

Is it

a _____

a _____

a _____

a _____

Let's look inside the box!

Writing frame (1)

How many stars?

10 _____ like _____

9 _____ like _____

8 _____ like _____

7 _____ like _____

6 _____ like _____

5 _____ like _____

4 _____ like _____

3 _____ like _____

2 _____ like _____

and 1 _____

like a _____

POETRY

How many stars? see page 51

Writing frame (2)

I flew into outer space one day.
Everything there came out to play.
There were

Ten spacecraft floating,

Nine rockets flying,

Eight comets_____

Seven_____

Six_____

Five_____

Four_____

Three_____

Two_____

and one lonely astronaut leaping
    along, up, up and away.

The sun, see page 55

Writing frame

The sun

The sun is like a _____

_____ing in the sky.

It is like a _____

_____ing _____

The sun is like a _____

_____ing across the clouds.

It is like a _____

_____ing _____

The sun is like a _____

_____ing up to heaven.

It is like a _____

_____ing _____

At the seaside, see page 59

At the seaside

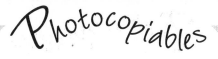

Opposites, see page 62

Writing frame

Day and night

In the day

_____

_____

_____

and the street is _____

In the night

_____

_____

_____

and the street is _____

Poems in colour, see page 65

Colour poem

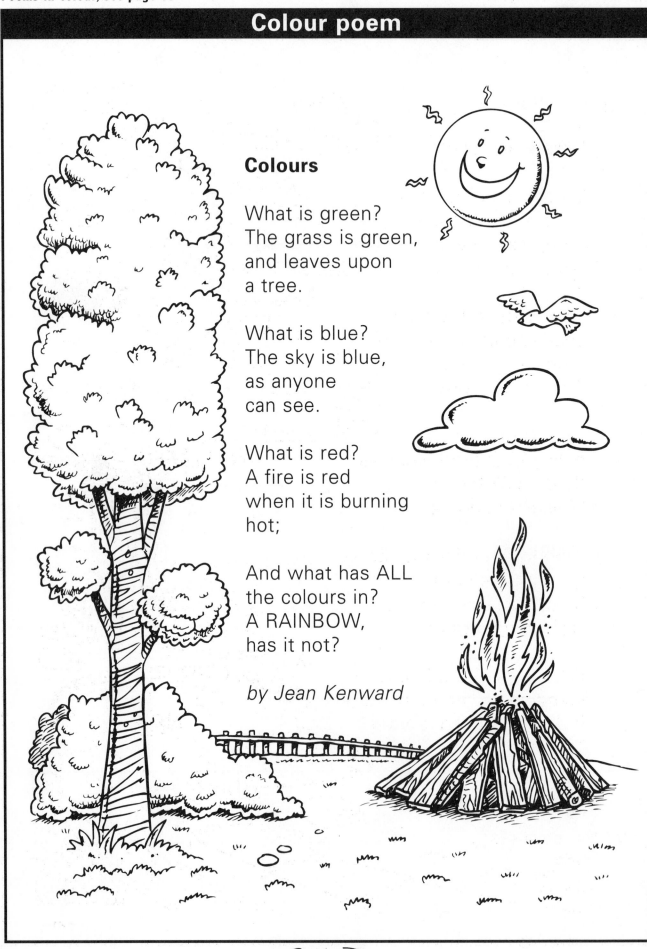

Colours

What is green?
The grass is green,
and leaves upon
a tree.

What is blue?
The sky is blue,
as anyone
can see.

What is red?
A fire is red
when it is burning
hot;

And what has ALL
the colours in?
A RAINBOW,
has it not?

by Jean Kenward

Pattern poem (1)

Who lives here?

Who lives in the web
hanging on the garden wall?
'I do,' said the spider,
'This is my home!'

Who lives in the pond
sparkling under the sun?
'I do,' said the fish,
'This is my home!'

Who lives in the nest
hiding in the old oak tree?
'I do,' said the bird,
'This is my home.'

Who lives under the stone
lying on the damp earth?
'I do,' said the beetle,
'This is my home.'

Who lives in the house
standing on the busy street?
'I do,' I said. 'I live here.
This is *my* home!'

by Moira Andrew

Who lives here? see page 68

Pattern writing frame (1)

Who lives here?

in a web?

in a hive?

_____

in a nest?

in a burrow?

_____

in a house?

_____

Pattern poem (2)

The Week

As gloomy as Monday
As chirpy as Tuesday
As half-way as Wednesday
As thoughtful as Thursday
As hopeful as Friday
As cheerful as Saturday
As restful as Sunday.

by John Cotton

Days of the week, see page 71

Pattern writing frame (2)

The week

As _____ as Monday

As _____ as Tuesday

As _____ as Wednesday

As _____ as Thursday

As _____ as Friday

As _____ as Saturday

As _____ as Sunday

In one second, see page 73

Pattern poem (3)

In one second

I can
    clap my hands,
    blink a bit,
    smile at my baby brother.

I can
    stamp my foot,
    poke out my tongue,
    shout at my little sister.

I can
    say I'm sorry,
    dry my eyes,
    give my mum a kiss.

by Moira Andrew

In one second, see page 73

Pattern writing frame (3)

In one second

I can

_____

_____

_____

In one minute

I can

_____

_____

_____

In five minutes

I can

_____

_____

_____

Five senses, see page 76

Pattern poem (4)

I like

I like the taste of toothpaste,
tingling on my tongue.

I like the smell of sausages,
nuzzling at my nose.

I like the feel of sunshine
flickering on my face.

I like the sound of bells
echoing in my ears.

I like the sight of fairground lights
flashing in the dark.

by Moira Andrew

POETRY

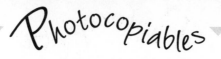
Pattern writing frame (4)

Five senses

I like the taste of _____

_____ on my tongue.

I like the smell of _____

_____ at my nose.

I like the feel of _____

_____ on my face.

I like the sound of _____

_____ in my ears.

I like the look of _____

_____

Countdown, see page 79

Pattern poem (5)

Countdown

There are ten ghosts in the pantry,
There are nine upon the stairs,
There are eight ghosts in the attic,
There are seven on the chairs,
There are six within the kitchen,
There are five along the hall,
There are four upon the ceiling,
There are three upon the wall,
There are two ghosts on the carpet,
Doing things that ghosts will do,
There is one ghost right behind me
Who is oh so quiet . . . BOO.

by Jack Prelutsky

Photocopiables

Countdown, see page 79

Pattern writing frame (5)

Countdown

There are 10 _____ in the _____

There are 9 _____ on the floor.

There are 8 _____ in the _____

There are 7 _____ behind the _____

There are 6 _____ in the _____

There are 5 _____ on the wall.

There are 4 _____ in the _____

There are 3 _____ in the _____

There are 2 _____ under the bed.

And one is _____

For the first time, see page 81

Pattern poem (6)

First Things

The first lick of the lolly,
The first bite of the cake,
There is something about them
You cannot mistake.

The first day of the holidays,
The first time you wear
Something new, then that feeling
So special is there.

The first time you open
A new comic the smell
Of the ink and the paper
Is exciting as well.

The very first bike ride,
The first dip in the sea,
The first time on a boat
Were all thrilling to me.

The first page of a book,
The first words of a play
And the first thing at morning
When you start a new day.

by John Cotton

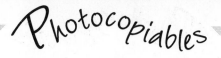
Pattern writing frame (6)

For the first time

I went to _____

for the first time,
    for the first time.

I saw _____

for the first time,
    for the first time.

I heard _____

for the first time,
    for the first time.

I tasted _____

for the first time,
    for the first time.

When the wind blows, see page 84

Pattern poem (7)

When the wind blows

When the wind blows
Coats flap, scarves flutter.

When the wind blows
Branches groan, leaves mutter.

When the wind blows
Curtains swish, papers scatter.

When the wind blows
Gates creak, dustbins clatter.

When the wind blows
Doors slam, windows rattle.

When the wind blows
Inside is a haven
Outside is a battle.

by John Foster

When the wind blows, see page 84

Pattern writing frame (7)

When the sun shines

_____

When the sun shines

_____

When the snow drifts

_____

When the snow drifts

_____

When the rain falls

_____

When the rain falls

_____

When the thunder roars

_____

When the thunder roars

_____

POETRY

My home, see page 86

Pattern poem (8)

Home

I am a pebble
Shiny red,
My home is on
The river bed.

I am a silver
Paper clip,
My home is on
A memo slip.

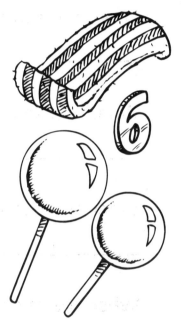

I am a yellow
Lollipop,
My home is in
The village shop.

I am a towel
With stripes of pink,
My home is by
The kitchen sink.

I am a golden
Twenty-four,
My home is on
An oaken door.

I am a kite
Of many hues,
My home is where
The wind should choose.

by Colin West

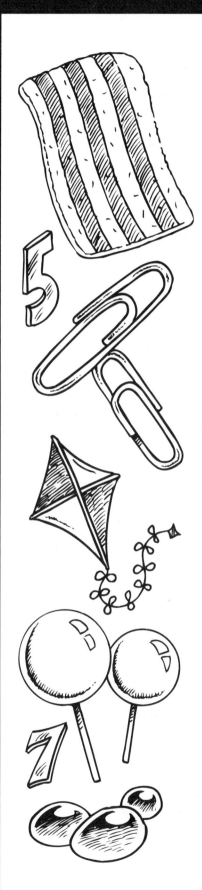

Acrostics, see page 90

Acrostics writing frame

F_____

I_____

S_____

H_____

T_____

I_____

G_____

E_____

R_____

D_____

O_____

G_____

S_____

ABC poems, see page 93

Alphabet poem

A–Z of beasts and eats

Alligators
bite
Coke cans.

Deer
eat
Fudge.

Gorillas
hunt
Ice-cream.

Jackals
kidnap
Lollipops.

Mules
need
Oranges.

Porcupine
quaver for
Rashers.

Serpents
toast the
Uneatable.

Vampires
want
Xtras.

Yoghurt's for
Zebras.

by John Fairfax

ABC poems, see page 93

Animal alphabet poem writing frame

A _____ as an a_____

B _____ as a_____

C _____ as a_____

D _____ as a_____

E _____ as an _____

F _____ as a_____

G _____ as a_____

H _____ as a_____

I _____ as an _____

J _____ as a_____

K _____ as a_____

L _____ as a_____

M _____ as a_____

N _____ as a_____

O _____ as an _____

P _____ as a_____

Q _____ as a_____

R _____ as a_____

S _____ as a_____

T _____ as a_____

U _____ as an _____

V _____ as a_____

W_____ as a_____

Xciting   as a xema

Y _____ as a_____

Z _____ as a_____

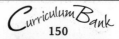

Recipe for a sandcastle, see page 101

Recipe poem writing frame

Recipe for a snowman

Take _____

_____

and _____

Add _____

_____

and _____

Stir in _____

_____

and _____

Decorate with _____

_____

and _____

And you have made a snowman!

Shape poems, see page 101

Shape poem (1)

Climb the mountain

see
blow,
you
against
wind
the
Feel
sky.
the
see
and
clouds
the
touch
high,
mountain
the
climb
Climb

t
h
e
f
i
e
l
d
s
f
a
r
f
a
r
b
e
l
o
w

by Wes Magee

Shape poem (2)

shower

fierce
  spring
    rain
        full
            gushing
              drain
drab   grey
  steely   puddled
   sky   street
      umbrellas   Wellies
         held   for
            high   feet
cars   children
  make   want
    spray   out
        birds   harassed
           huddle   mothers
              away   shout
rain   cats
  becomes lie
      drops   asleep
        slows   plants
          and   drink
            stops   deep
                doors
                  open
                    wide
                      people
                        step
                          outside

by Moira Andrew

Shape poems, see page 101

Shape poem (3)

Snow-stroll

I
love
the
snow
I
love
the
cold
I
love
the
crispy
patterns
my
feet
leave
behind
I
love
the
crunchy
sound
they
make
as
I
stroll
along
changing
direction
again
and
again
and
a
g
a
i
n

by John Walsh

Shape poems, see page 101

Shape poem writing frame (1)

I love the sun

bright

shiny

POETRY

Shape poem writing frame (2)

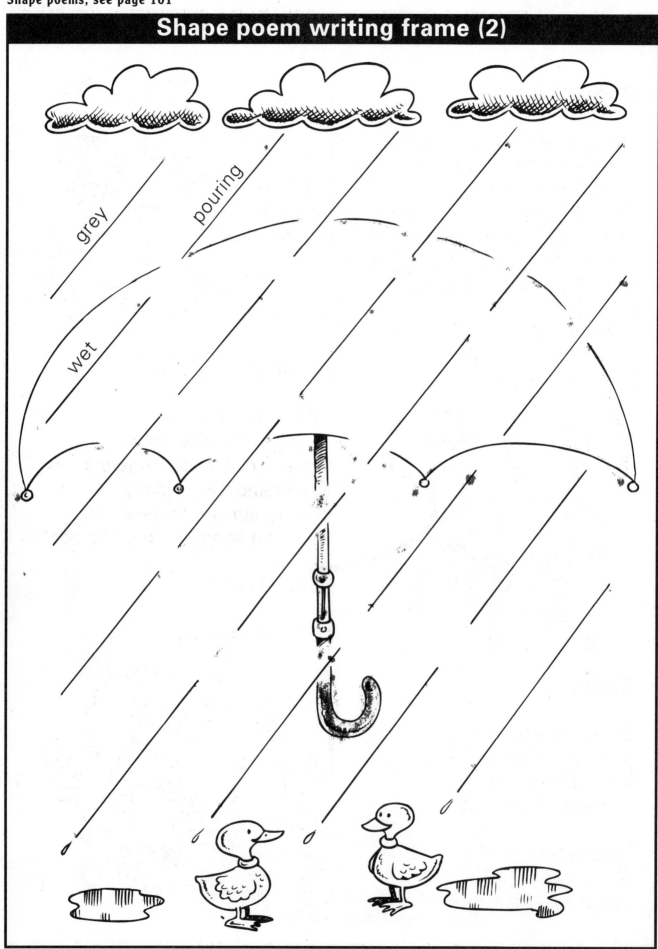

grey

pouring

wet

Riddles, see page 104

Riddle poems

Riddle of summer

I am a small iridescent twig,
Silver wrapped like a thin sweet.
A catch-sun, though you will not catch me.
Too quick as I skim the waters I came from.
When I pause on a reed or a lily's landing pad
I'm watching you, as you marvel.
You look again: I've gone!

What am I?

by John Cotton

Riddle of the pond

I shine like a jewel.
I flash across the pond
like an underwater firework.
I twist and turn, hiding
in deep-sunken forests.
Now you see me, now you don't.

What am I?

by Moira Andrew

Riddle

Brown speckled bird
feather-fluffed and fat,
with skinny pink legs
and a red party hat.

What am I?

by Moira Andrew

INFORMATION TECHNOLOGY AND POETRY AT KEY STAGE 1

The main emphasis for the development of IT capability within these activities is on communicating information, particularly through the use of word processing software.

Many of the poetry writing activities and extension ideas in this book can be used to develop children's IT capability through the use of a word processor. The teacher could organize children to do different writing tasks over a term or longer, some using more conventional written methods and others using the computer. This would also provide an opportunity for teachers to provide activities at different levels of IT capability, and to discuss with different children the relative merits of the use of IT for different purposes. Such an approach would be appropriate for independent group activities in the Literacy Hour. Where there is only one computer in the classroom, one or two children from a group could use it for a writing task.

Throughout Key Stage 1, pupils should be developing their confidence and competence in using word processing or simple desktop publishing (DTP) packages. Many word processors now have basic DTP features, and it may be possible to use a single piece of software for most writing tasks. A key difference between the two types of software is the way in which text is placed on the page. In a DTP package, text is generally placed inside a frame which can be altered in size and shape; the text is automatically reformatted to fill the new shape. This provides a flexible way for children to organize text and pictures on a page, and to experiment with different types of page design.

The children should be taught a range of basic keyboard and word processing skills. By the end of Key Stage 1, they should know the layout of the keyboard and where the letter and number keys are. They should be able to:
▲ make capital letters and characters found above the number keys using the *shift* key;
▲ use the *delete* key to erase text and to join lines together;
▲ use the arrow keys or the mouse to position the cursor;
▲ use more than one finger per hand when typing, particularly once they know where the letters are;
▲ use their thumbs to press the space bar;
▲ know that the word processor will automatically 'wrap' the text around the end of the line;
▲ go onto a new line by using the *return* key;
▲ select an appropriate font from a menu;
▲ alter the size or colour of a font (in single letters, words or lines);
▲ centre text using the *centre* command;
▲ add a picture to their work and position and resize it;
▲ move the cursor to a mistake and correct it without deleting all the text back to the mistake;

▲ print out their completed work (initially with support from the teacher, but eventually on their own).

The children will also need to save their work if they are unable to complete it in one session. They should be taught how to save a file onto a hard or floppy disk or a network, so that eventually they can do this without assistance. They will also need to be able to find and retrieve their work.

The children should be given opportunities to originate their work at the computer, rather than always writing it out and using the word processor to make a 'fair copy' for their folder or a display. It is often appropriate for children to make their first draft at the keyboard, save it, print it out and then redraft it away from the keyboard, thus giving another child the opportunity to use the computer. They can then return later to retrieve their work, edit it and format the final copy for printing. The developing drafts can be saved as evidence of the children's drafting and computer skills, and can even be included in a display to show how the work has developed.

Young children will take a long time to enter text at the keyboard, so it is important to ensure that the writing tasks are kept short and that, where possible, support is available to assist their computer use. Parents or other adults can often be useful for this, provided that they have the relevant skills and know when to intervene. Alternatively, they can be used (in longer tasks) for scribing, typing in the children's work and then working with them to edit and redraft it.

Many of the lesson plans suggest the use of framework files created in advance. These reduce the need for text entry, allowing the children to concentrate on new poetry writing skills or on the more sophisticated word-processing commands needed to edit, organize and present work for an audience. When such files are created, it is important to make sure that a backup is kept and that (where possible) the 'master' file is locked against accidental overwriting when the children save their own versions. The children also need to know where to find the framework files.

Where you have access to a large monitor or projector that can be linked to the computer, you can work with the word processor instead of a flip chart to show the children how drafting can be achieved at the computer. This would be an ideal way to introduce children to the potential of the word processor for drafting and crafting poetry. It also allows class poems to be created and edited as they evolve. As more primary schools have access to a computer room, this facility may become more widely available.

The children should be shown how to move the cursor around the text, and to delete and insert words or letters. They can also be shown how to move sections of text using the 'cut and paste' or 'drag and drop' commands. A useful method is to put unused ideas, words or lines at the bottom of a poem, so that they can be picked up later and inserted into the poem. This use of 'notes' can be applied to many word-processing activities.

IT links

The grids on this page relate the activities in this Curriculum Bank to specific areas of IT and to relevant software resources. The activities are referenced by page number. Bold page numbers indicate activities which have expanded IT content (in relation to a specific area of IT). The software listed is a selection of programs generally available to primary schools, and is not intended as a recommended list. The software programs featured should be available from most good educational software retailers.

AREA OF IT	SOFTWARE	ACTIVITIES (page nos.)			
		CH. 1	**CH. 2**	**CH. 3**	**CH. 4**
Communicating information	Word processor	18, 20, 23, 26, 29, **32**, 35, 37, 40	**48**, 51, 55, 57, 59, **62**, 65	68, 71, 76, 79, 81, 84, 86	**90**, 93, 96, 98, 101
Communicating information	DTP		59, 62		101
Communicating information	Art package	26, 29, **40**	48, 55	73	**98**
Communicating information	Drawing package				103
Communicating information	Authoring software			68, **73**	**96,** 104
Control	Tape recorder			68	

SOFTWARE TYPE	BBC/MASTER	RISCOS	NIMBUS/186	WINDOWS	MACINTOSH
Word Processor	Folio	Pendown Desk Top Folio Textease	All Write Write On	Word Write Away Textease Creative Writer	Word Easy Works Claris Works Creative Writer
DTP		Pendown DTP Ovation Textease		PagePlus Publisher Textease	
Art package	Picture Builder	1st Paint Kid Pix Dazzle	Picture Builder	Colour Magic Kid Pix 2 Microsoft Paint Dazzle	Kid Pix 2 Microsoft Paint Claris Works
Multi-media authoring package		Magpie Hyperstudio Genesis Textease		Genesis Hyperstudio Illuminatus Textease	Hyperstudio
Drawing package	Picture Builder	Draw Picture IT	Picture Builder	Claris Works Microsoft Draw	Claris Works Microsoft Draw

	MATHS	SCIENCE	GEOGRAPHY	ART	MUSIC	D&T	IT	RE/PSE
READING AND SHARING	Counting to ten, using number names and numerals.	Exploring the impact of weather on people and animals. Looking at the characteristics of food items. Discussing how smoke alarms work, and the uses of fire. Making and using a tin-can telephone. Discussing spiders' webs. Talking about nocturnal life in a forest. Investigating the sounds made by different objects.	Discussing how food items are harvested and transported around the world.	Representing a poem as a sequence of pictures. Adding collage materials to paintings. Finding different shades of a colour in magazines. Using charcoal and chalk to make a twilight picture.	Using choral reading to imitate the sound of a storm. Using words and actions to mimic kitchen sounds.	Making zigzag books with collage materials stuck onto the pages. Making a wall frieze. Making a 3D café display.	Word-processing poems, using different fonts, styles and colours. Using a prepared template file. Using the *tab* key to arrange text. Using clip art or an art package to illustrate text. Rearranging lines of text on screen. Formatting a poem on screen. Using colours, tints, shades and colour washes to modify a picture on screen. Scanning line drawings.	Talking about experiences of being lost. Talking about belief in magic. Talking about imaginary friends.
WRITING POEMS	Counting down from ten to one, using number names and numerals.	Discussing minibeasts and their homes. Looking at pictures of the night sky; discussing the moon and stars. Talking about the sun and sunlight. Examining natural objects such as shells, using the senses. Talking about shore life. Comparing day and night, summer and winter. Talking about colours in nature.		Making animal pictures for a frieze. Using spray paint and paper shapes (or 'wax resist') to create a night sky picture. Making accurate drawings based on observation.		Making a wall frieze with 3D features (insect wings). Making 'flames' from crêpe paper. Adding collage materials to a painting.	As above. Using a concept keyboard with a prepared overlay. Using a framework file with gaps for new text. Justifying the lines of a poem. Using a framework file with boundary lines for rows and columns. Using the *tab* key to place poems side by side on the page, or using the table facility to set up columns.	Talking about presents and the occasions when they might be given.
USING A PATTERN	Using the sequence of days in the week. Talking about how time is measured, and how long a second is. Counting down from ten to zero.	Talking about animal homes in nature. Talking about machines that measure time; using a stopwatch. Using the five senses to explore various objects. Discussing the effects of different kinds of weather on people and the environment.	Talking about people's homes in various countries. Discussing the places where various objects could be found.	Painting figures for a collage. Making a 'ghostly' frieze with black and white paper images.	Using percussion instruments to keep time with a steady beat. Identifying a percussion instrument by its sound; exploring words to describe musical sounds.	Making a collage from magazine pictures or from painted figures.	As above. Using a multimedia authoring package to create a talking book, and to create an electronic presentation of poems, pictures and sound effects. Using a DTP package to 'publish' a class anthology. Using the 'search and replace' facility to modify a repeated line in a poem.	Talking about the feelings associated with new experiences.
PLAYING WITH FORMS		Discussing the seasons and their effect on the natural world. Building up animal vocabulary. Using shape poems to explore weather.	Using shape poems to explore landscape and climate.	Drawing 'illuminated' capital letters. Working together to paint large pictures, with individual work added to form a collage. Using crayons or felt-tipped pens to write colourful shape poems.		Making bookmarks and corner cards to hold them in. Making a long zigzag book using all the children's work. Making paper streamers to display poems. Making riddle books with corner flaps to reveal the answers. Talking about recipes for cooking.	As above. Changing the font, size or colour of initial letters in an acrostic poem. Using the thesaurus facility of a word processor. Using a multimedia authoring package to make a book of riddles and their solutions. Placing text on the screen within an art package. Rotating text to print lines at various angles on the page, using a DTP program or drawing package.	Talking about holidays and festivals.

POETRY